The Home Adventure Library

Parents' Guide

By James Ertel
Illustrated by Ruth Rooney

Created by SYSTEMS FOR EDUCATION, Inc., *Chicago*
Published by THE SOUTHWESTERN COMPANY, *Nashville*

CONTENTS

NEW WAYS OF
LOOKING AT CHILDREN

THE GREAT GERMAN WRITER Johann Wolfgang von Goethe observed more than a century ago, "If children grew up according to early indications, we should have nothing but geniuses." Children are universally bright, and parents, grandparents, uncles, and aunts tell with pride the bright things that young children do or say.

"Indeed it is a queer thing that in babies and small children we welcome joyfully every sign of that intelligence we so much distrust in adults," said Clifton Fadiman. What happens to children along the way that they seem to lose this luster and this brilliance? Are adults united in a conspiracy to stifle the intelligence that every normal baby exhibits? Do our schools quench enthusiasm and kill curiosity? Do they foster a compliance that leads to adult mediocrity? Or do most of us simply not understand children, and thereby unwittingly force them into a confining mold that blunts their abilities?

In 1961, J. McVickers Hunt, Professor of Psychology at the University of Illinois, published what may well be one of the most significant books of this era, a book whose impact was still being felt throughout the educational community years later. This book, *Intelligence and Experience*, was a scholarly examination and reinterpretation of many of the child-rearing theories then in existence, and of the research data upon which these theories were based. In the conclusion of this highly important book, Professor Hunt wrote that evidence coming from studies about how animals learn, from medical experiments, from experiments with computers, and from observations of the development of intelligence in children has indicated that a new understanding of child development is needed. The assumptions that a child's intelligence is fixed and that it is determined by his heredity are no longer acceptable, Professor Hunt wrote. Then he added this crushing indictment of past attitudes:

"In the light of these considerations, it appears that the counsel from experts on child-rearing during the third and much of the fourth decades of the twentieth century to let children be while they grow and to avoid excessive stimulation was highly unfortunate."

Many writers since Hunt have called for a re-evaluation of the ways we rear children, and for a clearer understanding of children themselves. New findings from the field of neurology, which deals with the study of the brain, indicate that the early years of childhood are vastly more important than we have realized in the past and that much more can be done during this period to secure for the child a healthier, happier, more productive life. In 1966 the Educational Policies Commission, which was sponsored by the National Education Association and the American Association of School Administrators, issued a report which included the following statement:

". . . A growing body of research and experience demonstrates that by the age of six, most children have already developed a considerable

6

part of the intellectual ability they will possess as adults.

Six is now generally accepted as the normal age of entrance to school. We believe that this practice is obsolete. All children should have the opportunity to go to school at public expense beginning at the age of four."

In 1967 the noted child-care columnist, Joan Beck, whose advice is read regularly by 17,000,000 mothers, published a book entitled *How to Raise a Brighter Child*. In that book, Mrs. Beck reported on an enormous amount of research indicating that traditional child-rearing methods have, in fact, stifled children and stunted their intellectual growth. She reported also on many pieces of research that pointed out better ways of fostering intellectual development in children.

From other quarters has come information that many long-established notions concerning children simply are not true. The scholarly journal, *Exceptional Children*, has reported that, contrary to long-accepted belief, gifted children are not emotionally handicapped freaks who are good for nothing but reading books. Intellectually gifted children, reports this journal, tend to be bigger, heavier, healthier, and stronger than average children. They are more emotionally stable, adapt easier to new situations, tend to be more popular with their classmates, and are more self-directed and successful in their school activities.

On the other hand, studies from centers for the care of retarded children indicate that these children tend to be smaller, lighter in weight, weaker, and more prone to

illness than average children. They are more emotionally unstable, adjust with difficulty to new situations, and tend to have few friends.

The chapters that follow in this book reflect the newer attitudes which are coming out of studies about the development of children. These newer attitudes have already had notable success in Project Head Start, which, through 1967, had involved nearly two million children. These newer attitudes are the basis of what amounts to an educational revolution in which educational research centers across the nation are experimenting with ways to tailor the school curriculum to each child's individual capabilities and needs. These attitudes are the basis of new curriculum trends in which inquiry and discovery are substituted for memorization, and in which excitement takes the place of drudgery.

Not all of the ideas which underly the current re-evaluation of our methods of bringing up children are new. Some are as old as the ancient Greeks. However, modern knowledge is enabling us to interpret these ancient insights in a new light, and to understand more clearly what has been before us all along—our own children.

HELPING PRESCHOOL

CHILDREN GET READY

BILLY AND DAVID, two five-year-olds, started kindergarten on the same day.

The two boys lived across the street from each other in a fairly well-to-do neighborhood. Both boys had financially secure parents who saw to it that their children received proper medical attention and good nutrition. The parents of both boys were stable, industrious people who got along well together and who were well liked by their neighbors. The two boys were good friends and played together frequently.

But after school started, it very quickly became apparent that there were vast differences between the two boys.

David went to school not knowing the names of colors. He did not know that red was red and blue was blue, because no one had ever told him. He did not know how to color, because his parents never bought him crayons for fear he might scribble on the walls or the furniture in their well-

9

kept house. He did not know how to use scissors; no one had ever bought him any. David was the only child in the class who did not know how to read his own name. His parents had never taken the time to teach him.

Billy, on the other hand, not only knew all of the primary colors, but also the secondary colors, and many shades and tones like pink and lavender. Billy could not only read his own name, he could also write it. He could read simple books, too, because he had been widely exposed to reading at home. Billy could cut out fairly intricate shapes with scissors and paste them on paper. This was something which he frequently was allowed to do on rainy days when he could not go outside.

Within a month after the start of school, the teacher called David's mother and said that she would have to transfer the boy to the slow section of kindergarten because he was not nearly as "ready" as the other children in his class. David's mother was considerably shaken by the news, but her reaction was to announce throughout the neighborhood that she wished David's teacher was not so demanding.

For many decades in the history of American public school education it has been assumed—by parents, at least—that all students are educationally equal on the first day of school, and that what happens from then on throughout their educational careers depends on each child's mental endowment and how well he applies himself to his studies. This assumption has resulted in a tremendous amount of anguish, particularly for the children themselves.

Many carefully controlled studies, which were reported in the 1960's by Dr. Martin Deutsch, Director of the Institute for Developmental Studies and Professor of Psychiatry at New York Medical College, Dr. Robert D. Hess of the University of Chicago, and others, proved conclusively that all children are not equal on the first day of school, and that what happens to a child in the years *before* he goes to school has a tremendous bearing on his performance during his years *in* school.

Dr. Deutsch, for example, found that on the first day of school, slum children in New York City are not the equal of their middle class peers. Slum children are nearly one year behind their middle class counterparts before the formal educational process even begins. Nor is this gap made up. In fact, it becomes wider. By the end of third grade, slum children are about two years behind their peers, and by the end of eighth grade, about three years behind.

It is easy to imagine what must go through the mind of such a child. He must feel that the cards are stacked against him, that school is not the place for him because he has never experienced anything but frustration and defeat there, and that as soon as he reaches the legal leaving age he will get out. There is an enormously high percentage of drop-outs among these children, and they become the unemployables who account for much of the discontent that seethes in the ghetto areas.

Deprivation — Where and Why

Why are these children not equal to their peers on the first day of school? The biggest single reason is *deprivation*. The term "culturally deprived" has frequently been used to describe these children. True, they are "culturally deprived," but they are also sensorily deprived, nutritionally deprived, parentally deprived, and experientially deprived. Many slum children never see a book before they get to school, so they have no familiarity with books, and no real interest in them. Many slum children live in homes in which there are no pencils or other writing instruments, and so they have never learned to hold a pencil or to take any interest in the things that can be done with a pencil. Many slum children have never been more than a few blocks from their home. They are totally unaware of the animals in zoos, the sights and smells of a farm, the beauties in a museum, the sounds of a railroad station, or the things to see and examine in a quiet walk through summer woods.

The effects of deprivation are well known and well documented. The important thing for any parent to remember, however, is that deprivation is not limited to slum children. It can and does occur frequently in middle and upper class homes, too. It can occur in any home where the parents are too busy or too concerned with their own interests to take the time to see to it that a child has plenty of opportunities to see, hear, feel, touch, and explore new things and to be exposed to new experiences. Deprivation can occur in homes where parents feel that children are too ignorant to understand simple explanations, or where an alert child's questions are ignored or turned aside. Deprivation can occur in any home where parents do not understand the child's constant and insatiable quest for learning, his curiosity about everything in the world, and his tremendous ability to absorb information through his senses.

It is through his senses that every child must learn. Indeed, it is the only way that anyone, from infant to professor, can learn. Our senses are our only contact with the outside world, and every scrap of information that we acquire about that world must reach the brain through one or more of our senses.

The effects of deprivation upon children's developing brains are well known, and have been amply documented by a number of investigators. But what about the reverse process? What if, instead of depriving children of stimulation during these early years, we give them more than the normal amount? What, then, will be the result?

The Benefits of Enrichment

The results of an enriched environment during a child's early years are also becoming abundantly clear. People who have observed and written about children over the years have for decades felt that enrichment benefited children. Verification of this fact came in a number of studies which were conducted at universities during the 1960's. The facts are unmistakable and undisputed. A deprived environment results in a duller, less interested, more apathetic child. An enriched environment results in a brighter, happier, more interested child.

As Joan Beck reported in her book, *How to Raise a Brighter Child*, "Your child has already developed half of his total adult intellectual capacity by the time he is four years old and 80 percent of it by age eight. After age eight, regardless of what type of schooling and environment your child has, his mental abilities can only be altered by about 20 percent." Mrs. Beck was summarizing data presented earlier by Dr. Benjamin S. Bloom of the University of Chicago. The important point in this information is that parents and the preschool home environment are far more crucial in determining the child's academic potential than anything that happens to him in school—about four times more important, in fact.

The whole purpose of Project Head Start is to do things for preschool children that ought to be, but are not being done at home. Project Head Start has had proven success. In the first summer of this program, preschool children across the nation gained an average of nine I.Q. points in only six weeks, as a result of the mental enrichment which they received.

Enriching the Home Environment

Any home can be turned into an enriched environment for young children; only two things are needed. The first is an understanding on the part of the parents of the nature of the child's developing brain and an awareness of his urgent and compelling need to see, feel, touch, explore, and thereby learn as much as he can about the world. The second requirement is a willingness or an ability on the part of the parents to spend time with their children, not only in taking the children places to show them things, but in doing things with them, talking with them, and answering as clearly as possible their many questions.

One mother who took the time to teach her preschool child to read exclaimed delightedly, "I never realized before how bright he is. I have a whole new opinion of my child now as a result of this experience."

In addition to cultivating the attitudes mentioned above, parents can also do certain specific things to help enrich their children's environment. One of the most important things they can do is to make sure that children have plenty of opportunity for sensory stimulation. Children should be allowed to look at things, to feel them, to turn them over in their hands, to smell them, and, in the case of very young children, even to put them in their mouths.

Allowing children to do all of these things means, of course, that parents should take reasonable care to see that children do not get hold of things that might harm them or valuable things that they might break. However, if a child picks up an empty plastic ashtray, for instance, mother should not say, "No! No! Put that down!" It is obvious that the ashtray cannot harm the child, nor the child the ashtray. Rather, she should allow the child to look at it, feel it, taste it, and even bang it on the table (provided it won't hurt the table). What may seem to the parent a rather useless and wasteful activity actually is of tremendous importance to the child. Everything he learns about the plastic ashtray will be filed away in his brain, and will be used later to help him understand other objects.

When you open a can of coffee, let your child smell the rich aroma. If he wants to taste a dill pickle, don't tell him, "No, you don't want this. It's sour." Let him have a taste even though you know he will spit it out. When you put on perfume or hand lotion, put a drop on your little girl's hand, or let your little boy sniff the bottle.

If a child wants to see what is in a bag you brought home from the store, let him look, unless it is something that you want to keep as a surprise. Sometimes it requires patience to put up with children's constant exploring and investigating, but this patience is a sacrifice which parents should make cheerfully.

There are many interesting games you can devise to give vent to your child's urge for sensory experience. You can cut up squares of different kinds of cloth (cotton, wool, rayon, terry cloth, etc.), and ask the child to identify them by touch alone as he pulls them one by one from a bag. You can put different liquids in a number of small bottles, and play a game to see who can identify most of them by smell. You can play a game like "I'm thinking of something round and green that is in this room. Can you tell me what it is?" The child will have to look around and use his eyes until he finds something that answers your description. Then let him ask you a similar question. The number of simple games like these that can be done in the home with little or no preparation are almost endless, and they can provide the child with a great deal of sensory experience.

You can take the child outside the home on all sorts of inexpensive excursions which will provide him with a great wealth of sensory experiences and a tremendous amount of experience in coping with new situations. A later chapter in this book gives specific suggestions on how to get the most out of such an excursion. (See page 22.)

When Your Child Asks Questions

Answer your child's many questions patiently, and as best as you can. If he continually asks you things you cannot answer—and every child does—you can teach him how to find out answers to things he does not know about. You can say, "Well, I don't know the answer to that question, Sue. Let's look it up in the encyclopedia and see what that says." Use a children's encyclopedia, if you have one, because the answers in such a set are likely to be explained more simply. The important thing is that if the child sees you referring to books for the answers to questions, he will develop the same habit for himself when he is able to read.

Some questions—too many—cannot be answered simply enough for a child to understand. That is no reason, however, for you to tell the child, "You are too young to understand that. Your teacher will explain it to you when you get bigger." If your child asks you, for example, "What is electricity?" answer this question as best you can, or read him the answer from an encyclopedia, even though you know that he will not understand the answer completely. If you have at least tried to answer his question, it will prove to him that you respect his intelligence. Furthermore, you may be vastly surprised at how much he actually does understand. But even if he only understands a part of the explanation, he will have gained something, and the next time he has an experience involving electricity he will learn a bit more. Finally he will come to have a fairly clear understanding of what this strange force is.

When you attempt to explain a complicated subject to a child, you are exposing him to ideas. Therefore, he will be that much farther ahead the next time he hears the same words or is exposed to the same idea. Each new context will lead him to a greater understanding of the complicated ideas of modern life.

One very important thing you can do to provide your child with an endless source of enrichment is to read to him often. Books can expose your child to everything that man has thought, felt, learned, or done. An entire chapter on "Reading Readiness" appears later in this book.

DEVELOPING GOOD

ATTITUDES TOWARD SCHOOL

YOUR CHILD WILL SPEND at least 12 years in school. If he goes on to college, he will spend at least another four years. Graduate studies could take him two or more additional years. If he goes into medicine, he will spend a total of 20 years in school, plus additional years in internship and residency training.

Even after he finishes formal schooling, your child's education will probably not be complete. The knowledge explosion is proceeding so rapidly that for many people education will have to be a continuous process. Certainly this will be true for professionally trained people. Because education will be one of the most important factors in your child's life, it is important that he have a healthy attitude toward school, and certainly toward learning.

When it comes to instilling attitudes in children, nothing is more persuasive than the attitudes shown by parents. If, from the earliest days of your child's life, you express a healthy respect for and interest in learning, he will adopt your attitudes.

When your child starts school, his first reactions will be governed by various factors: his own ability compared with that of the other children; the prior preparation he has received at home; the nature of the school situation (whether it is warm and inviting or cold and forbidding); and the unconsciously expressed attitudes and expectations of his parents.

There is little that most parents can do about the school situation. Unless you choose to send your child to a private school, you will have to take whatever your public school has to offer. This is not too bad in most instances. In general, public school education has improved measurably over the last 20 years, although there are still localities where much more needs to be done.

But the other factors that determine your child's attitude toward school are within your power to influence. If you have taken the child outside of the home to see and do things, if you have read to him or perhaps taught him to read, if you have taught him the names of colors and how to use crayons and scissors, and if he has had experience in getting along with other children, your child should find the transition to school life easy and pleasurable. The famed Swiss child psychologist Jean Piaget said that the more things a child has learned to cope with, the more able he is to cope with new situations. Therefore, the more things that your child has learned to cope with before starting school, the easier it will be for him to adjust to the new situations he will face there. Also, if you have taught him to expect school to be exciting and rewarding, the better the chances are that this will be true.

Many of today's adults attended schools that were authoritarian and dictatorial. A great deal of time was spent memorizing multiplication tables, verb conjugations, and bits of poetry, simply because teachers insisted that this be done. As a result, many of today's adults did not like school, and they remember their school days as times when fear of punishment alternated with feelings of boredom.

Fortunately, many of the old pedagogical attitudes have changed in the last two decades. The new mathematics has taken the drudgery and memorization out of arithmetic and made it an exciting subject of discovery. Many new devices—film projectors of all kinds, recording machines, and manipulative devices—have brought excitement and immediacy into the curriculum. The old authoritarian attitude of teachers is giving way to an attitude of tailoring the learning situation to the individual child's needs and ability. Therefore, even if you remember your own school days with distaste, the chances are good that your child will not have the same reasons to dislike school that you did. If you did dislike school, put aside your prejudices—your child may find things entirely different.

When School Days Begin

Several months before it is time for your child to start school—whether it is nursery school, kindergarten, or first grade—start building in him a sense of expectancy toward the starting of school. Tell him that soon he will be old enough to go to school just as bigger children do (children always like to think of themselves as bigger and older than they are and to identify with older children). Tell him about pleasurable things that happened in your own school life.

Take your child on shopping trips to buy school clothes. Say, "This shirt (or dress) would be nice to wear to school. What kind of shoes do you think would be good for school?" If your child will have to take a lunch to school, let him select an attractive lunch box. Make sure that he gets any required medical examinations and shots. When you introduce your child to other adults say, "This is Jane. She will start school next September." The child will be pleased to be thought so grown-up.

The first day of school is a sentimental occasion in many households. It marks the transition from the home-centered life of the preschool child to the extra-home life which will be his from now on. Instead of making it an occasion for tears, treat the day as an exciting milestone. Take a picture of the child in his new school clothes, and dress up yourself, for this is an important occasion.

When you take your child to school on the first day, try to stifle any feelings of loss you may have. When you get to school on that momentous first day, in all probability you will not be presented with any problem of parting from your youngster. Most schools believe in a quick, clean break. After you locate your child's classroom, the teacher will probably give your child a cheery smile, shoo him into the classroom, and bid you an unceremonious goodbye. Most schools do not want parents waiting around on the first day. All you can do is go home and wait for your child's return, or wait until it is time to pick him up.

Schools do their best to ease the transition from home to school, and therefore the general practice is to make the first day as enjoyable as possible. Typically there are games, stories, and activities of one sort or another.

When your child returns home after the first day of school, and on succeeding days, he will probably be bubbling over with incomplete and almost incoherent accounts of what went on during the day. Listen to him patiently even if you are busy cooking chops or slicing carrots. After all, you have probably cooked hundreds of meals, but your child has only one first day at school. During these early transition days, be a good listener. Your child will have much to tell you, but there will be great gaping holes in his accounts that will leave you wondering just what did go on. Question him gently, but do not push or probe to find out everything.

Admire each drawing your child brings home, without pushing him to explain what it is. Many times your child may have started out with a specific idea in mind, but his skill proved inadequate to the task. Frequently he can recognize this fact. Therefore, you should just say, "Why, that's a beautiful drawing, Helen. I like the colors you used. Let's save this!" If the child then tells you, "It's a horse," say, "Why, of course, I can see that."

If there are tears or tantrums during those early days of school, try to learn the cause of them. Little Susie cried and said she did not want to go to school any more. It turned out that Susie thought her mother was sending her to school to get rid of her. As soon as Susie was convinced this was not so, she became perfectly happy at school. Robert did not like to go to school because, it was discovered, he did not like the harsh sound of the fire alarm bell. When he understood the reason for fire drills, he was perfectly content. Five-year-old David rebelled against kindergarten because, his parents found out, he was the only child in his class who could not write his own name. As soon as he could do this, his objection vanished.

Many of children's objections to school are trivial in parents' eyes but important to the child. That is why it is important to find out why your child objects to school, if he does, and to clear up the problem as soon as possible. If, despite your most patient questions, you are not able to learn the reason, by all means have a talk with the teacher.

Launching your child on his educational career is an important business. Your help in preparing him for this important step, and your warmth and enthusiasm in encouraging his early efforts, can be of tremendous help in making his career enjoyable and successful.

HOW TO PLAN

FOR AN EXCURSION

ONE OF THREE-YEAR-OLD Daniel's favorite activities was to line up the dining room chairs, climb on the first one, and pretend he was the engineer of a train. Daniel had ridden a train several times on trips to visit relatives in a city 200 miles away.

Then summer came, and Daniel flew with his parents in a jet to visit his grandparents in a more distant city. When he got back home, Daniel began arranging the dining room chairs in a different way. He put some in a straight line, and then put one chair at each side to stand for wings. Daniel was now the pilot of a mighty jet airplane.

Why had Daniel never made an airplane before? Probably because he had never been close to one, had never ridden in one, and had no real knowledge of what an airplane was like.

Much of children's imaginary play is related directly to their own experience. The broader their experience has been, the more things they have seen, the more things they are able to imagine.

Some workers with so-called "culturally deprived" children have noted that one striking thing about these children is that they appear to lack the ability to fantasize as middle class children do. Other workers in these fields have pointed out that this lack is probably not a lack of ability, but rather a lack of experiences about which to build fantasies. These children simply lack the mental lumber with which to build their dream houses.

To provide a child with the material for fantasies is not the only reason for exposing a child to new experiences, or even the most important one. More significantly, by exposing your child frequently to new sights, new sounds, new things, and new situations, you will be helping to satisfy his urgent need for mental stimulation. This stimulation in turn will directly affect the physical development of his brain, and make it possible for him to learn more. It is absolutely true that the more things a child has seen and heard, the more things he wants to see and hear, and the greater understanding he will draw from each new experience.

Many investigators have clearly demonstrated that children who are deprived of new experiences suffer mental defects much like those of mental retardation. Conversely, the work of the Institutes for the Achievement of Human Potential, in Philadelphia, of Project Head Start, and of other research centers has demonstrated that reversing this process—exposing a child to a great deal of sensory stimulation—can make the child brighter, and even cause him to score higher on I.Q. tests.

One of the ways you can expose your child to new experiences is through excursions to places he does not normally see every day. Good places to visit are zoos, parks, museums, firehouses, police stations, bakeries, airports, railroad yards, and even daddy's office. Farms, lakes, and forest preserves will also be new worlds for a city child. Each of these places contains sights, sounds, smells, and opportunities for motor experiences that will help satisfy your child's innate hunger for learning.

Planning an Enjoyable Excursion

Your child will get more out of one of these excursions if you plan it in advance and talk with him about it. If you are going to visit a historical site—say, Independence Square in Philadelphia—you and your child can read about what took place there, and why this site is so important. You can read about the men who met there, and look at pictures of the buildings and of the men who made history in them. You can talk about what life must have been like in those days, when there was no electricity, no radio, no television, no automobiles, and no telephones. You can talk about the things people used instead of these modern conveniences.

You and your child can prepare for a trip to a railroad yard by reading about trains—early steam trains and present day diesel and electric trains. You can talk about the different kinds of passenger and freight cars, and about how trains are controlled.

A visit to a museum can be preceded by sessions in which the family goes over the museum's guide book to determine what they want to see there. Most big city museums contain far more than can be seen in one visit, and using the guide book to plan the visit will help to make the trip more worthwhile. Let the child have a voice in choosing which things to see.

If you plan to visit a zoo, use books from your child's library to read about the animals that you are likely to see.

Perhaps he has books about animals, and favorites among the animals he has seen pictured. Ask him which animals he would most like to see.

When you go to the zoo, take an animal book with you, so you and the child can compare the pictures in the book with the animals you see. (Many of the illustrations in children's books are idealized or stylized. They may offend you, but they will not bother your child.)

Getting the Most from a Trip

While on the outing, the parent should be an unobtrusive, gentle guide. The main purpose of the outing is to benefit the child, and therefore the child's interests and inclinations should be respected. Mother (or father) should curb the constant impulse to say, "Come over here, Susie, and see the pretty indigo bunting." If the child wants to spend ten minutes looking at a boa constrictor, mother should try to check her impatience (and, if necessary, her fears). Parents can occasionally call attention to things the child might miss, answer questions, or volunteer interesting information, but they should not harangue the child or insist that he look at what they think he ought to see.

When you get back home, ask your child which animals or which things he enjoyed seeing most. You can then look these up in an encyclopedia, if you have one, and learn more about them. Encourage your child to talk about what he saw, but do not push him too much. Sometimes these experiences are too important and meaningful for a child to share even with his parents. You and the child can each draw pictures of the things you liked most about the visit or of the things that impressed you most. If you have gone to a museum, you can check off in the guide book the things you saw so that on a return visit you can make sure to see the things that you missed. Also, you can make notes in the guide book of things that you and the child enjoyed most and would like to see a second time. Again, the child can draw pictures of the things that interested him most at the museum.

To bring back memories of this and other trips, you can start a scrapbook. Inexpensive scrapbooks can be purchased at dime stores. You can ask the child to dictate to you a story about the trip. If he is not old enough to write, you can write his story and paste it in the scrapbook. If the child is far enough along in school, he should write his own account of the trip. Paste the story and any pictures that the child makes in the scrapbook together with a notation about the date of the visit. Each succeeding excursion can have its own page or pages in the scrapbook.

These preliminary and follow-up activities have several purposes. They make the actual experience more meaningful by preparing the child beforehand for what he will see. Another purpose is to ready his senses to respond to the new situation. The follow-up activities of discussion and writing in the scrapbook give him experience in putting into words things he experienced. Talking about the experience may make it possible for him to re-live it, and even to see in his mind's eye the same things he saw, to smell again the things that he smelled, and to hear again the sounds that he heard. All of these activities will tend to make your child more observant and more aware of his world.

Planning a Vacation Trip

One of the most important family excursions is the summer vacation trip. Many families travel to new places by car. If you are planning such a trip, go over with your children, well in advance, the route you will follow. For each area you will be passing through, find out about local historical sites or natural scenic features. You can find this

26

information in an encyclopedia or in the tourist maps and guide books supplied by oil companies and automobile clubs. You can write in advance to the local chambers of commerce or state recreation departments, asking for brochures, maps, and guides. Using all this information, you can have weeks of discussion about all the things that are available to see and what the various members of the family would like most to see.

Fathers can make a log book of where they will go, what they will plan to see at each stop, and where they will stop each night. Older children can learn to read highway maps, and figure out routes. When you get under way, let them be your "navigator," watching for road signs and highway markers.

Take your camera, of course, and plan your pictures carefully. Do not simply shoot a picture of mother and children against a pine tree somewhere, but try to arrange your photographs so that they will include some scenic or historical feature which will have meaning for the family later on. Also, if you have it, take along a portable tape recorder and tape any sounds that might have meaning for you in the future, like the sound of Old Faithful geyser or the mighty roar of Niagara Falls. Even the sounds of a busy downtown intersection in a large city can be exciting to children who live in a suburban or rural town. Ask the children to record on tape their impressions of the site as they are looking at it. If they feel free to do this in an unselfconscious way, it will be a valuable experience for them. But do not force this point if your children seem shy or unwilling to talk.

No one is suggesting that the preparatory and follow-up activities of a trip should be so rigorous that they will take all the joy out of it for the child. What has been presented here are simply some suggestions about things that can be done to make the experience more meaningful for both you and the children. You, as the parents, will have to decide which of these suggestions you will accept. It is recommended that you accept only those which you can do wholeheartedly and with genuine enthusiasm.

HOME PROJECTS

FOR YOUNG PEOPLE

EVERY PARENT HAS HEARD the childhood whine, "What can I do now?" This anguished plea is most likely to come on bad weather days when a child is cooped up in the house, or on days when illness keeps him from going out. But it can even be heard on beautiful days when there are no other children about, and the children at home have lost interest in their own toys and are looking for something new to do.

Parents should not be upset by this plea. It is the natural cry of an intelligent and inquisitive child who is seeking something new to learn or discover.

This chapter contains some specific suggestions for projects in drawing, painting, paper activities, and printing projects. Many hundreds of activities might have been suggested, but these particular ones were chosen because these activities make use of materials that are likely to be found in nearly every home.

28

Additional activities that are not discussed in detail here involve electrical projects, science projects, and home-making projects. Some of these, however, are a bit more complex, and many require things that might not be available in the house on unexpected rainy Saturday afternoons.

For example, there are dozens of electrical activities using harmless flashlight batteries and simple apparatus which can be done at home by a parent who knows only the rudiments of electrical circuitry. With flashlight batteries and a 3-volt motor, which can be bought in any hobby shop, it is possible for an inventive father and a creative child to conjure up all kinds of interesting new devices. A child will be intrigued to discover how he can light a flashlight bulb with nothing more than two batteries and a single wire. Switches, a buzzer, and batteries can involve a child in all sorts of safe yet fascinating experiments.

There are scores of home science projects involving such simple materials as seeds, tin cans, candles, and other things found in all homes. (Many books on science projects can probably be found in your local library.) However, as with the electrical activities mentioned above, science projects usually require that the parent have some rudimentary knowledge of the scientific principles involved.

Homemaking projects are numerous, and any inventive mother can, if she takes the time to think about it, come up with dozens that will interest a young girl, and many that will intrigue a boy. For example, a mother may tell a restless eight-year-old boy, "Years ago all mothers had to bake their own bread for the family. Let's try baking some bread and see what it was like." Look up a recipe in a cookbook and have an intriguing time watching the magic of rising bread. Making fudge, or pulling taffy, or stringing popcorn on thread are other activities that will intrigue youngsters.

Simple sewing projects will interest many young girls. An old family sampler, for instance, may make her want to try easy embroidery stitches. Scraps of leftover fabric—with encouragement from a mother who knows a little about sewing—can be turned into dresses for favorite dolls, curtains for a dollhouse, or many imaginative small gifts.

Around the holidays, children will probably welcome your ideas and help in making many of their gifts for others in the family.

Whenever the plea, "What can I do now?" comes, do not turn it aside. Unless you are hopelessly busy with other things, use it as an opportunity to explore some new activity that you and the child will both enjoy. The projects listed below are some simple ones that require no special knowledge or equipment.

DRAWING PROJECTS

There is a wide variety of things you can give your children to draw with. For a young child, it is better to select things that are easier for him to handle. For example, soft pencils are more rewarding than hard pencils to a small, inexperienced hand. Number 2 lead pencils are common in most homes and are soft enough. Wax crayon markers are also very good for beginners. They come in stick form with a string that makes it possible to peel off the casing to obtain more color.

Felt tip pens are very good for drawing, but be sure to get the washable, non-toxic, non-odorous kind. These pens come in many beautiful colors and respond easily to a child's touch. Ordinary wax crayons are always good, too. If possible, get a set of big crayons. Some art teachers recommend larger crayons because they feel the child draws more freely if given large tools.

There are many more tools a child can draw with: charcoal sticks, charcoal pencils, conté crayons, graphite pencils and sticks, and colored pencils. Charcoal is a magnificent medium. However, it can be messy and discouraging to someone who is too young to work with a light and controlled hand. But older children, who have better hand control, enjoy using charcoal.

If you give your child charcoal, start him out with the harder variety rather than the medium or soft. He ought to be supplied with a kneaded eraser for cleaning out small areas or spots, a chamois for erasing large areas, and a puff for blending in areas. It is also a good idea to give him a smock or apron.

To draw, your child will need something to draw on. Paper comes in many weights and finishes. A young child can do well with brown wrapping paper, paper bags, or the classified section of a newspaper. There are also inexpensive pads of paper called "newsprint" that can be purchased in an art supply shop. You can get inexpensive art papers at most dime stores. You can even buy wrapping paper from your neighborhood butcher.

Seven- to ten-year-old children enjoy experimenting with different materials. The papers available are many, varying from a hard glossy finish to a very rough, textured finish. An occasional trip to an art store can be a satisfying treat. There are, too, books an older child might find helpful. One basic book for anyone who enjoys working with a pencil is *Sketching and Rendering in Pencil*, by Arthur L. Guptill, who also wrote *Drawing with Pen and Ink*. Books by Joseph Pennell and Henry Pitz are also helpful to children who like to draw. These books can usually be found in any public library that has an art department.

Drawing involves the use of lines. Below are some projects that make use of such things as toothpicks, string, yarn, and stones as *tools* for making lines.

Toothpick Drawings

Materials: toothpicks, glue, construction paper,
      tweezers, pencil.

Arrange the toothpicks on the construction paper. Use the tweezer to place the toothpicks. When you have the arrangement you want, glue the toothpicks onto the paper. Pencil lines or small objects (seeds, stones) can be added to the drawing.

31

String Drawing

Materials: string, construction paper, scissors,
pencil, glue.

One way to make a string drawing is to do the drawing first in pencil and to follow the lines as you glue the string. Or, if you prefer, you can glue the string down freehand, not following a predetermined pattern. If you have them, use strings (or yarns) of different colors and thicknesses. Cut the strings at points where definite angles or breaks are intended.

Sandpaper and Yarn Drawings

Materials: coarse sandpaper, yarn, cardboard,
glue, scissors.

Glue the sandpaper onto the cardboard. Use the yarn to draw a picture across the sandpaper. The yarn will stick to the sandpaper, but it also can be pulled away if you want to make another drawing.

Stone Drawings

Materials: pebbles; cardboard, masonite, or wood; glue;
paint; brush; pencil

Paint the board the color you want for a background. Draw your design or picture with pencil. Work lightly. Fasten the stones in place with glue. You may prefer to work directly with the stones without making a pencil drawing. If so, it is a good idea not to glue down the stones until you have them all placed, because in a free approach such as this, it is helpful to keep the way open for making changes as you go.

Scribble Drawings

Materials: pencil, crayon, or pen; paper.

Use your writing tool to scribble with. Scribble easily and naturally. After you've scribbled for a while, look at the scribbles. See if you find anything in them. Some areas will suggest things to you. Outline these more heavily, or color them so as to make a mosaic of your scribbles.

PAINTING PROJECTS

If you think of painting as using areas of color, then you can paint in many ways. You can use bits of colored paper and make a paper mosaic. A variety of papers can be used to make a collage. A variety of fabrics will make another kind of collage. Stones and seeds can be used to make a painterly type of work as well as an outline drawing. In working directly with paint it is possible to use brushes, sticks, knives, or even straws to spread it around.

Paper Mosaic

Materials: colored bits of paper, paste (or rubber cement), construction paper.

The bits of paper are to be pasted on a sheet of construction paper. The idea is to create areas of color that form a pattern or picture. You may want to make a pencil drawing first.

Paper Collage

Materials: several kinds of paper, glue, pencil, scissors, cardboard or construction paper

A collage, like a mosaic, can be something worked out as you proceed, or it can take its shape from a drawing you make previously. If you make a drawing, then you will tear and fit into it pieces of paper that you have collected for the project.

Fabric Collage

Materials: scraps of cloth, glue, scissors,
board, needle and thread.

Collect an assortment of fabric textures that interests you. You can paste them on a board, cardboard, masonite, or wood. You can make a drawing first and select the fabric pieces to satisfy your idea of the drawing you have made. Or you can let the pieces of fabric lead you to a discovery of something as you work along.

You can also sew your pieces onto a piece of felt or muslin. You can use the stitches for special effects. Vary the color of materials, the color of threads, and the textures.

Straw Painting

Materials: construction paper, water paints (poster
colors), and soda straws.

Place a glob of paint on a piece of construction paper. Put one end of the straw in your mouth, and the other end of the straw to the paint glob. Blow gently. The stream of air spreads the paint about. Move the paper around and blow at the paint from several angles. Then put a glob of another color on your paper. You begin to get effects where the colors touch, blend, or border each other. Two or three colors are all you will want to use on any one straw painting. When you have finished, you can add ink lines to emphasize some idea you discover in the straw painting.

34

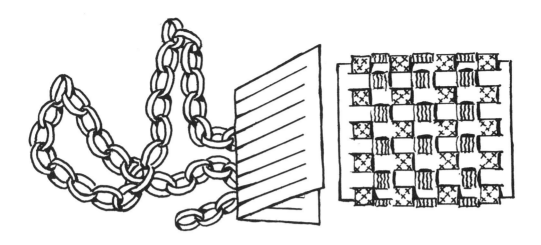

PAPER PROJECTS

Here are two simple projects that involve the use of paper.

Paper Ring Chains

Materials: colored paper, paste, scissors.

Cut paper into strips about 1/2 inch wide and 6 inches long. Make a circle (ring) of a strip. Paste it closed. Slip a second strip through the first. Paste it closed. Continue until you have a ring chain. Chains like this can be used to help decorate a room or table for a child's birthday party, or can be hung on the Christmas tree.

Paper Weaving

Materials: colored papers, pencil, ruler, scissors.

Fold a piece of colored paper in half. From the folded edge draw a series of ruled lines that are 1/2 inch apart. Do not draw them all the way to the open edge. You should leave a border of at least 1/2 inch. Cut along the lines from the fold to within 1/2 inch of the open end. Unfold the sheet. Next, select another piece of paper of a different color, and cut it into strips 1/2 inch wide. Weave these strips through the slits you have made. The first strip should slip *over*, then under; the next strip should slip *under*, then over. Continue to alternate strips in a weaving fashion. Variations can be achieved by making the slits further apart; by varying the width of strips you weave through, or by an interesting change of colors. Paper weavings can be used for place mats at a child's party.

PRINTING PROJECTS

Here are two simple printing projects that can be done with materials commonly found around the home.

Printing Gift-Wrapping Paper

Materials: 18 × 24 newsprint paper (or ordinary brown wrapping paper), paint or ink in shallow flat pans, sponges cut into shapes and glued onto a spool or block of wood, paint smock or apron, newspapers to protect the surface you work on.

Cut the sponges in definite and interesting shapes. These should be dipped into the paint or ink very gently. Do not dip them too deeply or you will lose the effect of the sponge in the design. However, each sponge must be dipped sufficiently so that its surface is covered. Apply the sponges to the brown wrapping paper, and repeat the design in a way that will make the overall print attractive.

Tin Can Printing

Materials: tin can, felt, string, burlap, wood, inner tube pieces (etc.), glue, poster paint, brush, paper.

Cut both ends from the can. Prepare the materials you will glue to the can; felt, string, burlap, pieces of wood, inner tube, or whatever you wish. Cut these into interesting shapes. Fit these pieces around the can, varying the size of the pieces and the distances between them. Do not clutter the can. The pieces are fixed on with glue. Paint the pieces with poster colors. Roll the can over paper, applying pressure with your hand inside the can.

READING READINESS

DURING THE 1700's AND 1800's in much of the United States, the teaching of reading was considered to be the responsibility of the home. Children were expected to know how to read before they came to school, just as they were expected to be toilet trained and to know how to put on and take off their own coats. Reading was considered not an educational activity, but a basic skill that made education possible. Teachers assumed that parents would teach their children this skill before sending them to school.

In the early decades of the 20th century, the pendulum swung completely the other way. Not only was the responsibility for teaching reading shifted to the schools, but school administrators actually urged parents *not* to teach their children to read. The reasons given were that parents were not as competent to teach reading as trained teachers were, and that they might "confuse" their children by improper instruction.

Some school administrators even warned that attempting to teach children to read before they were six years old could harm them. Children's eyes were not "ready" to read, said some educators, and neither were their brains. Too early an exposure to reading could cause psychological and emotional damage, it was said.

These warnings, which have since been proved groundless, possibly arose out of a sense of professional mystique on the part of educators. They were abetted by a profound lack of knowledge of what the reading process actually is.

Nevertheless, these warnings were heeded and had great effect. For most of this century, the teaching of reading has been considered the sole prerogative of the schools. Though there has always remained an "underground" of early readers, many parents still believe the old, dire warnings, and deny their children the gift of reading even when these children want to learn.

However, in the 1950's and 1960's, psychologists, scientists, and some educators began taking a different view of the abilities and learning capacities of very young children. They discovered the real harm that could come from withholding opportunities for learning.

Teaching Preschoolers to Read

In the first half of the 1960's, a few educators and scientists began urging parents to teach their preschool children to read. One of the most articulate of these was Glenn J. Doman, Director of the Institutes for the Achievement of Human Potential, who in 1964 published a book, *How To Teach Your Baby To Read*, in which he urged the teaching of reading to children as young as two years of age or possibly even younger. Doman also published a kit of materials for parents who wished to teach their young children to read. Another set of preschool reading materials was published by Mrs. Dorothy Taft Watson. Doman and Mrs. Watson were roundly criticized by some educators—and warmly praised by hundreds of parents who used these materials and did teach their preschool children to read.

One professional educator who advocated early reading was Dr. William Fowler, Director of the Nursery School at the Laboratory School of the University of Chicago. Dr. Fowler published several scholarly papers in which he described the methods by which he taught his own children to read in their preschool years. Another professional educator who urged the teaching of reading to preschoolers was Professor O. K. Moore, of Rutgers University, who developed a $400,000 "talking typewriter" that was highly successful in teaching very young children to read.

Doman's arguments in favor of the early teaching of reading were varied and startling. He stated that learning ability varies inversely with age, and that it is actually easier to teach a four-year-old to read than a six-year-old. Doman insisted that, in neurological terms, learning to read is precisely the same process as learning to hear and understand spoken language. Any child who can learn to understand a spoken language can also learn to understand a written language, Doman said. He also proclaimed that parents who had the experience of teaching their children to read would come to have a greater respect for their child's ability to learn and would actually enjoy their children more.

Studies of Early Reading

Educators judged many of Doman's arguments to be subjective and therefore incapable of proof. However, many hundreds of letters that he received from delighted parents indicated that their respect for their own children did grow during the process of helping them learn to read.

Similar feelings were reported by hundreds of parents who followed a preschool reading program published in comic strip form by Joan Beck in the *Chicago Tribune* and syndicated to other newspapers around the country. This feature, based on the work of Mrs. Watson, drew more favorable responses from its readers than any other promotional feature that the *Tribune* had previously published.

In 1966 a long, definitive study into the effects of early reading was published by Columbia University Press. The author was Dolores Durkin, and the title of her book was *Children Who Learn To Read Early*. Through reading tests which were administered to first graders at the beginning of school, Dr. Durkin identified 49 children in Oakland, California, who came to school knowing to read, and 156 more children in New York City. Dr. Durkin made intensive studies of these children including their socio-economic background, mental age, number of siblings, and other factors. She matched these children with other children who had similar characteristics, and followed the progress of the test groups and the control groups through six years of school. What she found was that children who came to school knowing how to read were already ahead of their classmates, and that they tended to stay as far ahead even through six years of school.

In the concluding chapter of her book, Dr. Durkin wrote as follows:

"When the initial study began in 1958, it was rather generally assumed that early readers would have problems later. The predictions took a variety of forms, most often one of the following: beginning too soon, early readers would be bored later; or, learning from someone not trained to teach, they would later be confused.

The findings in these two studies in no way corroborate the pessimistic predictions about the future achievement of early readers. Even after six years of school instruction in reading, the early readers, as a group, maintained their lead in achievement over classmates of the same

40

mental age who did not begin to read until the first grade."

In 1962 the famed Harris School in Chicago began teaching reading to three- and four-year-olds in junior kindergarten. After four years of this program, the Headmaster, Warren Wadsworth, reported that out of a total of 120 children who had been exposed to the reading program in junior kindergarten, all had learned to read. No child had failed to learn.

Wadsworth is proud of the success these children have achieved in school. He reports that, in 1967, the first grade students at the Harris School scored a median of grade 2.4 on the Stanford Achievement test. The second grade students scored a median of grade 3.7. Other private schools in the Chicago area are following the lead of the Harris School, and have taken up the teaching of reading in junior kindergarten.

A Continuing Controversy

The controversy regarding early reading is not over, and perhaps never will be. Nothing dies more slowly than an ancient belief, and the belief that teaching preschoolers to read could cause harm was a deeply ingrained one. Furthermore, there are a sizable number of parents who simply do not want to be bothered, although frequently they will not admit this fact even to themselves. Many professional educators have changed their opinion on the matter, but many more of them still continue to oppose the idea.

What you, or any parent, should do in the face of these uncertainties is to decide for yourself. And, in reaching your own decision, probably your attitude about teaching your child is the most important thing to consider. If you can go about teaching your child to read with the relaxed attitude that if the child learns, all right, and if he doesn't, all right, then it would be a good idea for you to teach him. But if your attitude is one of tenseness and fear of failure, it would probably be better not to attempt to teach your child to read. If you take pleasure in seeing your child learn, then you should not deprive yourself of the pleasure of seeing him learn to read. If you do not ever like to see your child fail at anything, then you would be better off not teaching him to read.

Methods of Teaching Reading Early

Should you decide to teach your child to read, the method you use is probably unimportant; certainly it is far less important than your own relaxed and trusting attitude. The methods which have been used with success to teach preschoolers to read are many and varied. They range from the $400,000 talking typewriter of O. K. Moore, which is built around a complex computer, to the simple hand-lettered word cards advocated by Doman in his book. The researches of Dolores Durkin as to how the children in her studies learned to read indicate that they learned by various methods. In some instances the preschool child was taught by an older brother or sister who had learned to read in school. In some cases, the preschoolers themselves initiated the reading activity, and kept pestering their parents with questions about "What does this word say?" She reported, too, that some children became interested in reading as a result of learning to write.

Dr. Maria Montessori had reported earlier, in 1949, that she had found that many young children became interested in reading as a result of teaching themselves to write.

42

Probably the easiest methods to use at home are the ones recommended by Doman and by Mrs. Watson. Both of these methods have been used successfully by thousands of parents. Doman's method stresses visual discrimination. Simply put, this means that you begin with very large printed words which are easy for the child to see and recognize. As he learns to read, the size of words can be decreased gradually. This is basically the same method used by Dr. Fowler. The kit which Doman published contains a number of words printed in red letters, in four-inch type. Each successive group of words is printed in smaller type, until the child actually begins working with printed books. Complete details of this method can be found in Doman's book mentioned above.

The method used by Mrs. Watson is based on phonics, which stresses the relationship between letters and the sounds that the letters stand for. It is basically a translation method. The child learns to translate printed letters into sounds.

Despite the many arguments pro and con concerning these two methods, there is no firm evidence that one method is any better than the other. Much depends on the age of your child when you teach him, on the way your child learns best, and also on your own attitude towards these two methods. If you feel more comfortable or confident using one than the other, choose that one.

If you do decide to teach your child to read, do so with the idea that you are doing something that is for his benefit—not for yours. Do not teach your child to read simply to show him off to the neighbors, or to make him "smarter" than another child. Bear in mind that the evidence is clear that learning to read in the preschool years can be a tremendous benefit to your child in later years. So it is your child and his needs which should determine the nature of the instruction.

Do not push and pressure your child to learn to read, and do not use bribes or threats once you have started to teach him. The use of force or pressure in teaching a child to read is one of the things that educators strongly oppose, and in this objection they are right.

Of course, it is not possible to raise a child without some pressure. Everything that parents do in the way of disciplining a child or teaching him anything involves some pressure. Toilet training, for example, involves the use of parental pressure, but few educators would urge parents not to toilet-train their children. Similarly, teaching a child the everyday common courtesies and the small skills like washing his face or tying his shoes also involves some pressure. The teaching of reading need not require even this much pressure if it is treated as a game or a reward by parents. As Doman points out, you want to associate reading with pleasure in the child's mind, and so you should never make the teaching of reading a forced or painful chore.

Some educators assert that young children have no interest in reading. This is certainly not universally true; many parents know that their children are curious about words and books, and what words say. But even if a child demonstrates no interest in reading, the parents still can attempt to teach him to read. Few people have an interest in things they know nothing about. A person who knows nothing about baseball, for example, probably has little interest in it. Conversely, if he learns something about baseball, then he will develop an interest in it. Too often we forget that interest develops as a result of the ability to do something rather than the other way around. Even children who seem to have no interest in reading develop this interest quickly as they begin to acquire the ability to read.

Doman's advice that learning to read should be made a pleasurable activity is valuable, and should be kept uppermost in your mind when you start to teach your child. A parent who heeds this advice will probably not use too much pressure in working with his child. Faith and patience are also helpful. Remember that your child did not learn to understand spoken language overnight, but you accepted it as a certainty that he would learn to hear, understand, and speak language. When he was a baby you talked to him even though you knew he could not understand all that you said. However, by constantly being surrounded by talk, gradually your baby did learn to understand. The same basic process

44

works for reading, too. Your child will not learn to read right away, but if he is frequently exposed to reading, he will learn to read just as surely as he learned to understand the words you speak to him.

Give Your Child Reading Experiences

Even if you decide not to attempt to teach your child to read, there is a great deal you can do to make learning to read easier for your child when he goes to school. And on this point there is no argument—reading is the key to success in school.

The most important thing you can do for your child is to read to him. Take him in your lap at quiet times during the day or at night before he goes to bed, and read him a book that he enjoys. Nearly all children have favorites that they like to hear over and over again, but you should encourage him to want to hear new books read, too. When you read to your child, read slowly and clearly, and with warmth of feeling. If your child points to a word and asks you what it says, tell him. These warm, happy times of reading together will help your child associate reading with pleasure.

Let him see you reading—and enjoying it. Let him see books and magazines as a natural part of his world, and of yours. Parents who seldom or never read will have difficulty in convincing their children that they should read. If you have gotten out of the habit of reading, or if you never did do much reading, now is a good time for you to cultivate the reading habit. Children are great imitators, and if they feel that you take pleasure in reading, they will naturally assume that they will too.

In the comic strip *Pogo*, there appeared a bear who wrote poetry. He had to ask others to read his poetry to him, though, because, as he explained, his mother taught him to write but never taught him to read. This notion is not as ludicrous as it sounds. Many children who cannot read are nevertheless very much interested in writing. One of the finest reading readiness activities you can provide for your child is pencil and paper, and his name printed in large letters. Nearly every child is deeply interested in his own name and will practice for hours to learn to write it. After he learns to write his own name, he will probably ask you how to write the names of other family members, and then other words. These activities will go a long way toward preparing your child for successful reading instruction when he gets to school.

Leave the cereal box in front of your child's plate when he eats breakfast. In all probability he has seen television commercials showing that cereal, and very likely he can read some of the words on the box. Encourage him to do this, and read to him any other words on the box that he asks about. Also read him whatever words appear on favorite toys or records, or other boxes and jars of food.

In short, even if you do not choose to teach your child to read, you should expose him to *reading experiences*—for it was through exposure to language that he learned to understand spoken language, and it is through exposure to written words that he will ultimately learn to read. The sooner this exposure begins, the better, and the easier it will be for him to learn to read.

MATH READINESS

IT IS STARTLING to realize that the preschool child of today will live more than half of his productive life after the year 2000.

Dr. Jack E. Forbes, Professor of Mathematics at Purdue University, has pointed out that no one can say positively what that century will be like, but almost certainly it will be more of a "mathematical world" than is our world today. Forbes and others have predicted that all that is known in the fields of science and mathematics today will probably constitute no more than ten per cent of what will be known in the year 2000. About one-half of today's preschool children will spend their lives working at occupations that do not even exist today.

Because of the rapidity of change, it is no longer sufficient for a child to memorize the facts of the past. The multiplication tables which today's adults memorized when they were in school are still *true*, but they are not enough.

Today's child needs to learn the basic structure of mathematics so that, as the field changes, he can change along with it.

There is much that you can do to give your child a good background for mathematics, even if you disliked it in school and "never really understood" it. This chapter contains some suggestions for specific activities that will be fun for both you and your child.

What Is Counting?

Most children start school already knowing how to "count." That is, they can repeat the sequence: "one, two, three, four, five, six, seven, eight, nine, ten." To most children, however, this is simply a series of noises which, if repeated in the proper order, bring an approving smile from mother. Five-year-old Linda was counting on the fingers of one hand, "One, two, three, four, five," she said, "and four is hurt." There was a bandage on Linda's fourth finger. She had confused ordinality and cardinality, which is common for young children, but which can cause great trouble later in attempts to understand mathematics.

Even if your child can "count," *i.e.*, repeat counting words, there is no reason to assume he knows what these words mean, unless you have made it a point to teach him. But before you start teaching him to count, it would be better to demonstrate to him what counting actually means.

The best way to begin is to teach your child what a "set" is. *Set* is a word that is used in modern mathematics to refer to a *collection* of things. A football team can be considered a set, for instance, as can the trees on your front lawn, the members of your family, or the socks that your child puts on in the morning.

Teach him that a set is simply a bunch or collection of things, and use the word often so he will get the idea clearly. Tell him, "Here are some cookies. We call a bunch of things like this a *set*." Point out to him that he and his playmates are a *set* of children. Ask him to put a *set* of knives, forks, and spoons on the table for each person at dinner time.

Comparing Sets: More, Fewer, Same Number?

After he has absorbed the idea of a set, which should not take long, teach him to compare sets to determine whether two sets have the same number or whether one has more or fewer than the other. This activity is very simple. It amounts simply to pairing objects in one set with those in another to see whether each object in one set can be paired with an object in the other set, or whether one set has some objects left over. For example, you can put two sets of cookies on the table and play a game to determine whether both sets of cookies have the same number. Line up the two sets of cookies so that a cookie in one set touches a cookie in the other. If each cookie in one set touches a cookie in the other set, the two sets have the *same number*. If there is one or more cookies left over in one set, that set has *more*, and the other set has *fewer*.

Similarly, your child can match the set of fingers on one hand with the fingers on the other. Touching each finger of one hand to a finger of the other will prove to him that the two sets have the same number. You can point out to him that in the table setting there is one cup for every saucer, and so there are the same number of cups as there are saucers. Do not at this point get into the idea of "how many." That will be the next activity.

Teaching the Names for Numbers

After your child has learned what a set is, and has learned to determine whether two sets have the same number, more, or fewer, you can go into the idea of what *number* is. *Number* is simply one property of a set of objects. It is the answer to the question "How many?" We can ask many questions about a set. For example: What are they? Cookies.

What color? Brown. Are they sweet or sour? Sweet. How many? Four. The answer to the question "How many?" is always a number. The marks we use to represent numbers are called *numerals.*

Working with cookies, buttons, clothespins, or any other small objects, and an empty box, you can begin to teach your child about numbers. Keep in mind that you want to teach your child to learn to count *things*, and not merely to learn a series of words.

Starting with a set of buttons, for example, place one button in the box and say, "There is *one* in the box." On a piece of paper about two inches square, write the numeral 1 and put it beside the box. Tell your child, "This numeral says one."

Then remove the button from the box and put in a clothespin. Again tell the child, "There is *one* in the box. Here is the numeral that says one."

Take out the clothespin and tell the child to put one button (or one cookie, or one sock, or whatever) in the box.

If he does not put one in the box, do not show any disappointment. If he does nothing, wait for a few seconds, and then you put one in the box and tell him, "There is one in the box." If he puts more than one in the box, tell him, "No, there is more than one in the box." Empty the box and repeat the previous activities.

It may take several brief sessions before your child understands clearly what *one* is. It is important that he understand this, because all of the succeeding activities will be based on a clear understanding of *one*. When your child clearly understands what *one* means, you are ready to proceed to the other numbers.

Start with a set of buttons, and, as before, put one in the box and then place beside the box the numeral 1. Then put one more button in the box and tell your child, "There is one in the box, and one more. That makes *two*." Write the numeral 2 on a piece of paper and place it beside the box in place of the numeral 1. Tell your child, "This is the numeral that says two." Repeat this activity using other objects, and then place two pencils in the box. Ask your child, "How

50

many pencils are in the box?" If he answers correctly, praise him warmly. If he does not, do not scold or show any disappointment. Simply repeat the activities in several brief sessions until he understands *two*.

Teach *three* just as you taught *two*. Put one button in the box and tell him, "There is one in the box, and here is the numeral that says 1." Then add another button and say, "There is one in the box and one more. That makes two." Replace the numeral 1 with the numeral 2. Then add one more button and say, "There are two in the box, and one more. That makes three." Place the numeral 3 by the box.

After your child understands *three*, teach him the meaning of *zero*. (Please use the word "zero" rather than the words "none" or "nothing.") Start with three buttons in your hand and put one into the box. Say, "There is one in the box, and here is the numeral that says 1." Then ask your child, "How many are in my hand?" If he answers you correctly, praise him warmly. If he does not, say, "I have one and one more in my hand. That makes two." Then move another button from your hand to the box. Tell your child, "We have one and one more in the box. That makes two, and here is the numeral that says two. How many are left in my hand?" After he answers you, put the last button in the box. Say, "We have two and one more in the box. That makes three. Here is the numeral that says three." Then add, "There are zero buttons in my hand. Here is the numeral that says zero." Write the numeral 0 and place it by your hand.

Now begin taking buttons out of the box one at a time and returning them to your hand. When the box becomes empty, tell your child, "There are zero in the box, and here is the numeral that says zero."

Teach your child the numbers four through nine just as you taught him the others. Be sure to teach him the appropriate *numeral* each time you teach him a new *number*.

Teaching Numbers above Ten

When you get to ten and the numbers above ten, the important thing is to make it clear that all of the numerals for these numbers are constructed from the numerals 0 through 9. You should help him understand that we group by tens, and that two-digit numerals stand for sets of ten plus so many more. For example: the numeral 11 stands for one set of ten and one more; the numeral 45 stands for four sets of ten and five more.

To get this idea across, you can use sticks and a rubber band. For example, you can work up from zero, as before, and when you have ten sticks in the box you can say, "Now we have so many sticks that it is hard to keep track of them, so let's group these together into one set." Take the sticks out of the box, put a rubber band around them, place the banded set on the table, and put a numeral 1 by it. Tell your child, "This means we have one set of ten."

Then put one stick in the box and a numeral 1 beside the box. Tell the child, "There is one in the box." Remove the single stick from the box and place it by the banded set of ten. Bring the two numerals together to form the numeral 11. Tell your child, pointing to the numeral on the left, "This means we have one set of ten." And then pointing to the numeral on the right, "And this means we have one more." This method makes it possible for the child to see that the numeral 11 means one set of ten and one more.

Spend enough time on the idea of grouping by tens so that your child comes to understand thoroughly that 23 means two sets of ten and three more, and that 32 is three sets of ten and two more. Using buttons, paper clips, or other small objects, you can have hours of fun on rainy days doing number game activities. For example, give your child a handful of paper clips and ask him, "How many more will you need to make 34?" Encourage him to group the paper

clips by tens so that he will be able to determine how many more paper clips he needs to arrive at the required number.

Why Learn Mathematics?

Make sure that your child comes to understand that mathematics is not a series of abstract concepts, but rather a tool we use to talk about the real world. You can do this very simply and naturally during everyday activities. For example, ask your child, "How many knives do you need to set the table for the whole family?" "How many cars are there on the street in front of our house?" "How many pans are on the stove?"

If you treat mathematics as a natural part of human expression, your child will not be confused by this subject when he gets to school. If you have given him an opportunity to learn what numbers really mean, his school work in mathematics will simply be an extension of what he has already learned at home.

The activities outlined above should be done over a large number of very brief periods. They can be done on rainy days or at times when your child is bored and says, "What can I do now, Mommy?" Such a time would be a good time to play "a number game."

As mentioned in the chapter "Reading Readiness," do not push or pressure your child to learn. You will not have to. If you simply expose him to these activities in a pleasant way, you and he will both enjoy them.

A QUIET STUDY CORNER

TEN-YEAR-OLD FREDDIE hung his head and looked at his shoes and the crack in the classroom floor while his teacher scolded him for not having brought in his homework. Everybody else in the class had brought in his homework, said the teacher, and there was no reason why Freddie should not have finished his.

Freddie could feel his ears turning red while the teacher talked. There was a very good reason why Freddie could not do his homework, but Freddie would never have told the teacher what it was. Freddie simply had no opportunity to do his homework. He lived in a small apartment with his teenage sister, a younger brother and sister, and his two parents. His teenage sister had her own small bedroom which she guarded jealously, never allowing Freddie to come in. Freddie slept in a larger bedroom with his younger brother and sister, but they went to bed early and the lights were put out. Freddie had to stay out of the room until it was time for him to go to bed. His mother had spent the evening in the living room with the television turned on loudly, while his father sat in the kitchen, arguing with a neighbor about the local baseball team. There was no place for Freddie to go, so he huddled quietly in a corner of the sofa, watching television until his mother sent him to bed.

Freddie was one of those all-too-common children in our modern crowded urban society—the child with no place to go, the child with no sanctuary. Freddie had not done his homework because there was no place at home where he could do it.

Everyone needs a place, a corner, a spot that he can call his own, where he can keep the things that are important to him. This is true for adults and probably even more so for children. A child needs a place where he can have privacy, solitude, and an opportunity to do both the things he wants to do and the things he needs to do (such as homework).

In most households with two or more children, the children have to double up on bedrooms. Even so, it is still possible to figure out ways for each child to have a private space that is his alone. If there are two or more children in a bedroom, bunk beds can conserve space so that there is room for each child to have his own working area. If the family lives in a house with a basement, it is possible to finish off a portion of the basement at low cost, and arrange working space there. In apartments, a corner of the living room or the dining room (often unused except at mealtimes) might be set aside as a child's area. Few homes are so crowded that it is not possible to find some space that can be reserved for each child.

Furnishing a Study Corner

Whatever area you select to be your child's own, fix it up to be as functional and attractive as possible.

Get a decent desk, even if it is a second-hand one, and a comfortable, child-sized chair to go with it. Make sure there is ample light that can be controlled by the child himself. Put a bookcase or bookshelves nearby (you can build

inexpensive bookshelves with bricks and plain boards painted an attractive color). Add some thoughtful extra touches, too. A bulletin board is cheap to buy or to make. Inexpensive chalk boards can be hung at a proper level for the child to use easily. Having his own pencil sharpener, a real one like they use in school, will be a thrill to the child. It can be bought inexpensively at an office supply store. A small file cabinet might be handy to store those precious drawings or papers he brings home from school.

If you have made the effort to prepare a comfortable corner for the child, then he should be required to keep it orderly. Before he goes to bed at night, everything should be neatly put away—pencils in the holder, books on the shelf, and papers in the drawer. Children of certain ages tend to be "collectors." With boys, you will have to allow for a certain number of boyish treasures like broken door knobs, odd marbles, stray pieces of chalk, nails, a stick or two, and fragments of broken toys. Don't demand to know *why* they have to save these things; just grin and bear it. Girls will want to save their own treasures—photographs, postcards and letters, a tattered book, a broken but still loved doll, or perhaps a stuffed animal minus a leg and an ear. Arrange for a drawer to contain these treasures and agree that you will never intrude into his domain.

Your Child's Own Library

Begin the habit of book collecting by providing your child with the foundation of a good basic library. Begin with the dictionary appropriate to his own age level. There are beginners' dictionaries, junior dictionaries, dictionaries for high school students and for college students and adults. Your bookstore will be able to provide you with a dictionary that is appropriate for the age of your child. An encyclopedia and an atlas also belong in your child's basic library. Encyclopedias are available in a broad range of prices and qualities. Ask your child's teacher or a librarian what she would recommend in your price range for your child.

Also provide your child with basic books about the earth, nature, animals, famous people, famous places and other basic subjects. By all means do not forget his own particular sphere of interest. If he is interested in dinosaurs, for example, there are scores of books available on the subject at low cost. So that your child can feel proud of his very own library, let him put bookplates in his own books or write his name on the flyleaf of each one.

INTRODUCING YOUR

CHILD TO THE LIBRARY

VICKIE AND TOM were pulling on their snowsuits, boots, and mittens to go with their mother on a trip to a neighboring suburban shopping center.

"Get your books." said Vickie to Tom. "It's time to take back our old books and get some new ones."

The high spot of the weekly shopping trip for the children was to stop at the branch library, return the books they had taken out the week before, and spend an engrossing half-hour or so selecting books to take home for the week to come.

Vickie and Tom's mother had introduced her children to the library when they were toddlers, and it had always been a special place for them. They were fascinated by the rows of books, and they had learned to find their way to the particular sections that interested them most.

The library habit is one of the best habits you can cultivate in your children. There is no arguing with the fact that this is an age of information. The ability to acquire and use information is becoming increasingly more important. Libraries are repositories of information, and already heads of libraries are making plans to utilize computers and communication lines to make all of the information in all the libraries in the country available to any single library.

If you would cultivate the library habit in your children, you must begin by cultivating in them the reading habit. Read to them when they are very young, and let them see you reading books and enjoying them. Begin early to take them on trips to the library to select books. Get them library cards so that they may check out their own books.

Create the basis of a home library for each child. (See the chapter on "A Quiet Study Corner.") Make it clear that there are certain books that the child will own, which are his alone, and that there are other books—those in the library—which he shares with other people.

Teach your child to obey library rules, particularly those of returning books on time and of showing proper care for library books. Make your children understand that the reason for returning books on time is to let others enjoy them. Paying a fine for an overdue book is not an expiation of the offense. Actually, it costs most libraries more to collect and process the fine than the fine itself amounts to. Library fines are used only as jogs to get people to return books so they may be kept in circulation. Teach your child to respect library books, and never to mistreat them. He should never write in them, or tear out a page, or even turn down a corner to mark his place.

You need not give your child an intensive course in library science, but you can get him to understand that a library is actually a number of collections of books. If a boy is interested in dinosaurs, you can tell him, "Well, I think that books on dinosaurs would be in the section for animals. Let's find out where that section is and go look." Once he comes to understand the grouping system which libraries use, he will be better able to make fuller use of the library. You can also use this grouping system to introduce him to new areas. You might surprise him one day by saying,

"We've never looked in the art section. Let's go see what they have there."

Once children become familiar with the cataloging system in your library, they will find going to the library less confusing and more exciting. The girl who is interested in dolls or costumes will be delighted to find the sections where these books are located. The boys who are interested in space flight or snakes will be happy to browse in these sections. From time to time encourage your children to go on exploring expeditions in the library to see what new things they can come up with.

Expose your children to the card catalog and explain that by looking through the cards they can learn about all the books that are available in the library on a certain subject.

Most large libraries have special rooms or sections containing books for children and young people. Don't restrict your children's "world of books" to just this section, though. Show them the reference section, and the periodical section in the library. Many libraries also have music rooms where recordings and music can be taken out just as books are. A few libraries even have film sections.

Trained librarians are expert at finding the answers to questions. If a child asks you a question that goes beyond the resources of your home library, tell him, "Well, let's remember that and see if we can find the answer when we go to the library on Saturday." Let the child ask the reference librarian his question, and let him watch as she goes about finding the answer.

Libraries are a valuable community resource just as a school is. You will be doing a great favor to your child if you teach him to use and respect the library facilities that are available to him.

HELPING YOUR CHILD

DEVELOP GOOD STUDY HABITS

MANY PARENTS AND CHILDREN—more particularly parents, if their children are in the early years of school—are concerned over the relationship between good grades and success of one sort or another. Certainly it is true that a number of studies have indicated that there is a statistical relationship between good grades in school and financial success in later life. However, this seeming relationship may be spurious. It may have nothing to do with *how* a particular child studies or *how* he earns his good grades, but may depend basically on how intelligent he is to begin with.

In addition to the pressure to get good grades to ensure future success, there are other forces operating on children to compel them to try to achieve high marks.

One pressure is a belief that a child must get good grades in order to get into a decent college. This is far less true than most parents and their offspring realize. College admissions officers now take into account a great many factors besides grades. Another kind of pressure comes from parents who desire their children to earn good grades out of a sense of familial prestige. Some such parents even bribe their children with promises of cars or foreign travel if the children can get listed on the honor roll. Teachers or school administrators sometimes apply pressure for good grades so the class or school record will look good. Still another pressure for good grades, particularly for high school and college students, comes from the desire to avoid or postpone military service.

All of these reasons for obtaining good grades—and for developing good study habits in order to obtain them—are quite unrelated to what are commonly considered the basic goals of education. Parents, who should be wiser in discerning motives than their children, should be wary of pressuring for scholastic excellence simply for the sake of the reasons stated above.

The most valid reason for a child to develop good study habits is to enable him to be self-directed and self-sufficient in his ability to learn. For more and more people, learning is becoming a continuing process, not one that is limited to a certain period of his life. The need to know how to study and learn is becoming a life need, not simply a temporary skill to meet the school situation.

A prominent educator who became president of a respected Eastern university was not able to graduate from high school, even though he spent five years trying. He failed in a public high school and was expelled. His distressed parents sent him to private schools, which also expelled him for scholastic failure. Even though he had never gotten a high school diploma, the young man was provisionally admitted to a college because his father was a close friend of the director of admissions. In college, the young man distinguished himself scholastically, was elected to Phi Beta Kappa, and went on to earn a doctoral degree.

Although his high school grades never indicated it, this young man had probably developed good study habits. It so happened that in high school he applied these habits to subjects that interested him rather than to things that his teachers wanted him to study. This case is unusual but nevertheless pertinent, because his good habits, when applied in the greater freedom of the college curriculum, produced dramatically successful results.

It is fairly easy for authoritarian parents to make sure that their child will develop what they think are "good study habits." All that the parents need do is to insist that the child study every night from 7 to 9 o'clock, for example, and to enforce this rule with rigid and uncompromising rigor despite tears, pleas, or excuses. Such a regimen will probably make certain that the child will study, but it probably will not make him like studying nor, by extension, learning in general. For the child's future well-being, it is far more desirable that his parents cultivate in him an enjoyment, or at least a willingness to study, rather than force him into it against his will.

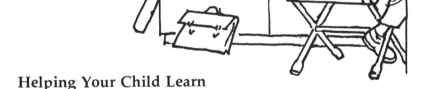

Helping Your Child Learn

One very important thing that parents can do to help their children develop good study habits is to provide them with a definite place to study. By doing this, the parents will be effectively demonstrating their recognition that a child's studies are important, just as father's work at the office is important, or mother's responsibilities for running the home. (Specific suggestions on how to set up a study corner are contained in the chapter on page 54.)

The development of good study habits can be approached by the "back door"—the things which a child is already eager and willing to learn more about. Encourage your child in his special interests. They may seem to be mercurial and to change from one month to another, but parents should respect them, nevertheless. Answer your child's questions as best you can. If you do not know a triceratops from a stegosaurus, ask him to explain to you what the difference is. Buy him special books about water filtration, early Chinese rockets, Indian tribes, or whatever else has strongly aroused his interest. If there are museums nearby that will help him learn more about things he is interested in, take him there. Make him realize, however, that even though you respect his interest in this particular subject, it is also important that he spend enough time on the subjects that his teachers think are important.

You can even apply the "curriculum enrichment" plan at home. Good teachers like to introduce supplementary activities or material to make the basic textbook program more interesting. Parents in their own ways can supplement the basic school program at home. If your child is studying in school about the Pilgrims, you can get an entertaining book about their life from the library and read it to him at story time or before he goes to bed. If your child is learning about how plants grow, you can equip him at little cost with a small window-box garden at home, and let him plant his own seeds.

The Problem of Homework

What about helping your child with homework? Ordinarily children in the early grades, for whom this series of books was designed, are not given much in the way of homework. However, some schools do believe in introducing the homework idea early as a means of helping to develop a sense of responsibility.

Authorities differ on the amount of help that parents should give their children in doing homework. Some warn that the parents' way of doing things may be different from the way things are done at school, and that this difference may tend to confuse the child. Certainly this warning is justified in the case of parents who do not know the new math. They would be likely to flounder helplessly if they tried to help a child who is studying this seemingly strange new brand of arithmetic. Teaching materials and techniques have changed quite a bit in 20 years, and it is entirely possible that parents will be bewildered by the things their children are learning and the way they are learning them.

There is another side to the issue, however. Sometimes parents, because they know their children so well, are better able to explain a difficult concept than a busy teacher who has to deal with 25 or 30 other children. In such circumstances, the help of a parent can be a great value to the child. It is patently obvious, however, that the parent is not really doing the child a favor by doing the child's homework for him. Helping the child to understand things better so he can do his own homework is quite a bit different from doing the homework for the child.

If your child asks you for help with his homework, or if it is apparent to you that he needs help, do your best to act as a tutor, not as an academic crutch upon which your child leans in order not to have to do his own work.

Some parents are too tense and impatient to help their children with homework. If you find yourself becoming ill tempered or cross with your child while attempting to help him understand long division, slow down and ask yourself what is wrong with you.

If you have any serious questions about the advisability of helping your child with homework, by all means ask the child's teacher for a conference and discuss the matter with her. In some cases teachers welcome the interest and assistance of parents. In other circumstances the teacher may advise you not to try to assist the child.

WHAT TO DO WHEN

THINGS GO WRONG AT SCHOOL

DANNY WAS THREATENED with being expelled from school at the tender age of ten. He was failing half of his subjects, and doing poorly in the rest. Also, for months his teacher had been sending notes home complaining that Danny was a severe discipline problem; he was disrupting the entire class.

In a conference with the teacher, Danny's mother was told that when the boy was asked to stand and read from his book, he would simply refuse to do so. When the class was asked to copy something from the blackboard, Danny would make paper airplanes and sail them around the room, walk to the window, or start poking one of his classmates.

Danny's mother found these reports hard to believe. At home, Danny was a quiet, well-mannered, obedient, and respectful child. His mother simply could not believe that he was such a hellion in school until she accepted the teacher's invitation and hid in the cloakroom to observe her son's behavior. Then she could hardly believe what she saw. Danny did everything that his teacher said he did.

His mother went from one type of counselor to another, seeking aid for Danny. Nothing seemed to work. She considered sending him to a military school in hopes that rigid discipline would cure his misbehavior.

After some months, however, it was discovered that Danny was suffering from a minor but disabling form of minimal brain dysfunction that made reading nearly impossible for him. When this problem was properly treated, Danny's grades zoomed, and his misbehavior stopped.

A New View of Troubled Children

During the 1940's, 1950's, and much of the 1960's, it was common to assume that there must be a psychological basis underlying the behavior of children such as Danny. (In fact, one of the counselors who advised Danny's mother made much of the fact that she had been divorced. This was the root of Danny's problem, said the counselor.) To a generation fed on Freud and made anxious by Adler, all problems that could not otherwise be explained were believed to be psychological problems. The fact that not all problem children responded to psychological counseling did not cast doubt on the efficacy of such counseling; it was rather assumed that in such cases the problem was so deeply buried in the psyche that it had not yet been discovered.

Beginning with the last half of the 1960's, however, professional journals began to present research articles dealing with "minimal brain dysfunction," "dyslexia," and "perceptually handicapped children." Countless symposiums and workshops were held. The pioneering neurological works of Dr. Carl H. Delacato, Director of the Institute for Learning Disability at the Institutes for the Achievement of Human Potential, and of Dr. Newell Kephart of Purdue University began to be much discussed and debated. Dr. Curtis Benton, an ophthalmologist from Fort Lauderdale, Fla., reported in 1966 that his seven-year research indicated that somewhere between 5 and 15 per cent of all children are suffering from dyslexia, which he defined as a reading problem that is not caused by a lack of intelligence. Dr. Sam D. Clements, Associate Professor, Department of Psychiatry and Pediatrics, University of Arkansas Medical Center, reported after considerable study that he estimated that 18 per cent of school children were suffering from minimal brain dysfunction. A new view of troubled children was emerging.

Learning Problems = Discipline Problems

As of 1968, it was beginning to be recognized that the problems that children usually have in the primary grades of school are usually either learning problems or discipline problems. More often than not, the two exist together in the same child.

It not infrequently happens that a child who is suffering from an undiagnosed learning problem is constantly pressured by his teacher and his parents. If he has older or younger siblings who are doing well in school, the pressure becomes even worse. He is told, "Nancy and Norman are doing very well in school, and we know you are just as bright as they are. You just aren't trying." Because of this repeated pressure, the child frequently does develop an emotional problem. At this point the school psychologist might say, "This child has an emotional problem. That's why he can't learn." Dr. Delacato has reported that he used to send such children to a psychiatrist. "What I got back were happy, well-adjusted reading problems," he stated. Educators are now coming to realize that an emotional problem is more often the *result* of a learning problem than the *cause*.

In the vast majority of cases, children who are disciplinary problems in school usually are also below-average students, or are performing at levels below those which their parents and teachers expect. Occasionally, however, it happens that a brilliant or gifted child also becomes a disciplinary problem. Very often the root of such a child's problem is boredom. The curriculum is not challenging enough to keep him interested and busy, so he devises special activities for himself which sometimes disrupt the class. Many school districts have special classes for above-average children, in which they are permitted to move ahead at their own speed and are properly challenged by an enriched and more demanding curriculum.

If your child has problems in the primary grades, it is important to try to clear them up while he is still young and the problems are easier to handle, and before he gets into the upper grades where his scholastic record becomes far more important. As a first step, discuss the matter with the child to see what his version of the problem is. It may be some simple thing like being afraid of fire drills, or not being able to play ball as well as the other children at recess. If, however, the child puts all the blame on the teacher, on the school, or on the other children, you should not accept uncritically everything that he says.

If the conference with the child does not settle the situation, the next step is to ask for a conference with the child's teacher, and possibly with the principal. If the child is both a disciplinary problem and a learning problem, the first thing to attack is the learning problem. Usually when this is cleared up, the disciplinary problem also disappears,

because children who are doing well in their school work are not normally unhappy or rebellious children.

There are a number of things that can cause learning problems in children, and you should investigate all of the possible causes.

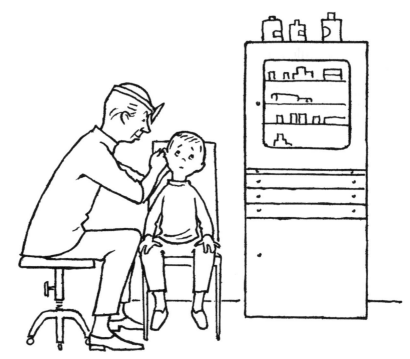

Possible Physical Causes

Some of the potential causes are physical. It may be, for example, that the child is suffering from an undiscovered illness. Take the child to his doctor for a thorough checkup to make sure that he is not suffering from rheumatic fever or some other debilitating ailment.

Have his eyes tested by an optometrist or ophthalmologist. In most schools, children's vision is tested by the school nurse using a Snellen chart. This is the famous chart with the big letters. In this test, the child covers his left eye and, from a distance of 20 feet, reads letters on the chart with his right eye. Then he covers his right eye and reads with his left eye. If the child successfully passes this test, the assumption is made that his vision is normal and that he is functionally able to read.

70

But it is now recognized that this assumption is totally unwarranted. A child can pass the Snellen test superbly and still have serious vision defects that can cripple him as a reader. Reading from books, which is what the child is required to do in most of his school work, is done not at a distance of 20 feet but at a distance of approximately 13 inches, and with both eyes working together, not one at a time. Many children, particularly in the lower grades, have difficulty converging their vision at this short distance, and, as a result, they see double images or foggy, imprecise ones. They never think to tell the teacher or their parents about it because they assume that this is the way *everyone* sees close up. Such a problem, however, can cause a child incredible difficulties in trying to read. A thorough eye examination will reveal if the child does have any such problem. These functional visual problems can usually be corrected.

Another thing to check is the child's hearing. Hearing problems are less common than vision problems, but they do exist, and they can cause great difficulty for the child. Once again, this is the kind of a problem that would not be evident to the child or even to the parents, but can easily be detected by a competent doctor.

Psychological Problems

Emotional or motivational problems can also cause learning difficulties. A child who is constantly compared in a disparaging way with a brother or sister or with a neighbor's child may, in effect, simply give up the struggle. Similarly, a child who is told often enough by his parents that he is "stupid" will sooner or later come to believe it and will act this role accordingly. Some minority group children feel there is no sense in their struggling to learn, because even if they do succeed in school, they will not be likely to "get anywhere" once they are out of school.

Sometimes parents, by discussing the situation calmly with each other or with the teacher, can discover an apparent emotional or motivational problem and take steps to correct it.

There are occasional psychological problems which can prevent children from performing adequately in school, though these problems are probably not so common as it was once believed. Sometimes, however, stresses within the family do lead to psychological problems. If there is constant bickering between the parents, with resulting tension in the home, the child will sense the tension and very likely be affected by it. Children from broken homes have been known to blame themselves for the divorce and to punish themselves accordingly. Jealousy over a brother or sister can also put so much stress on a child that it impairs his abilities to study or concentrate. Some of these problems must be handled by a trained professional. An interview with the teacher, with the school psychologist, or with the guidance counselor may be of help in determining if such a problem exists.

Neurological Problems

There is a growing belief, however, that the majority of learning problems, particularly in children in the early grades, are caused by what the National Institute of Health has termed *minimal brain dysfunction*. This term is used to describe the child who seems to be otherwise perfectly normal yet who cannot learn. It is applied to the child who has a normal or above-average I.Q. and yet cannot learn to read. It is applied to the hyperactive child who appears totally unable to concentrate for more than a few seconds at a time. Many of these problems, it is now recognized, are actually brain problems.

People who study the learning process realize that only the brain can learn. But the brain is an incredibly complex organ which is not fully understood even by neurologists. However, intensive study into the functioning of the brain has been going on at hospitals, universities, mental institutions, and schools across the country since the end of World War II. Much has been discovered. It is now known that children who are suffering from minimal brain dysfunction can be helped, many of them dramatically. Cases have been recorded of children who were originally diagnosed as retarded but who, after a period of treatment, actually proved to be gifted.

There are a number of signs which *may* indicate that a child is suffering from minimal brain dysfunction. The signs to look for are the following: (1) the child is of normal or above average intelligence yet he seems unable to learn; (2) he has a strabismus (crossed eyes); (3) he exhibits retarded speech; (4) he is physically uncoordinated or clumsy; (5) he is hyperactive and unable to concentrate; (6) he is subject to sudden outbursts of temper, and (7) he does well in mathematics and art, but does poorly in reading and other subjects that rely heavily on the printed word.

The presence of one or more of the above symptoms in a child does not necessarily mean that he is suffering from minimal brain dysfunction. It does mean, however, that such a possibility exists and should certainly be checked out.

Many school districts have trained personnel who are capable of working with children with minimal brain dysfunction. Other districts do not yet have such workers. If you have reason to suspect that your child may be suffering from this handicap, and if his school does not have the resources to help him, ask among doctors or clinics in your area for the name of someone who is trained in this field. Many of the larger cities now have clinics which are devoted to working with children suffering from minimal brain dysfunction. Most of these clinics have very good records of success.

HOME DISCIPLINE

A FATHER AND HIS YOUNG daughter were walking through the park on a warm spring day. Suddenly the little girl let go her father's hand and dashed off to examine a delicate spring flower. Her father called her back.

"Sally," he said, "I want you to stay on the path."

A little farther on, the girl again ran away over the grass. Her father called her back sharply.

"Sally," he said sternly, "I told you to stay on the path."

When the child dashed away a third time, the father's irritation exceeded his endurance. He ran after her, grabbed her by the arm, and spanked her smartly. "I told you to stay on the path!" he said through clenched teeth.

The little girl looked up at him with tears running down her cheeks. "Daddy," she said, "what's a path?"

This story illustrates one of the biggest breakdowns in what is called "discipline"—lack of understanding. The child did not understand the word "path," and the father did not understand that her "disobedience" was simply lack of understanding.

Therefore let us hoist high a banner with the word UNDERSTANDING emblazoned on it as the key to child discipline. Since parents are older, bigger, stronger, and presumably more knowledgeable than children, it is parents who will have to do most of the accommodating in this task of mutual understanding.

What Is "Disobedience"?

What precisely is meant by discipline or "obedience"? Is the child who dumps his mother's sewing basket on the floor so he can examine all of the wonderful things in it "disobedient" or "undisciplined"? Possibly he is, or possibly he isn't.

If he has performed this act several times before, has been punished or admonished, and has been told clearly not to do it again, then quite obviously one would say that the child is disobedient. If, however, no one has ever told him not to do this, and if the sewing basket has been left invitingly within his reach, then just as obviously he is not being disobedient. He is simply satisfying his normal, insatiable curiosity.

We have to realize it is not necessarily the act itself that determines obedience or disobedience, but the child's motivation in performing it.

There are factors which govern children's actions which frequently do not apply to adults. One of the most important of these is the desire to feel, touch, and examine every new thing. This is a compelling force which leads children into all sorts of difficulties with their parents, even though the children mean no harm or disrespect to their parents in obeying this force. Another factor in what is sometimes called disobedience or "naughtiness" is simply lack of judgment. A child may not have learned that in climbing on the piano, he runs the risk of falling off and hurting himself badly, or that in running his fingers over a sharp knife he can get a serious wound.

Why Children Should Obey

Children's curiosity and lack of judgment are the bases of a number of valid and compelling reasons why children should be commanded to obey their parents. Among these reasons are the following:

To prevent harm to the child. The world is full of dangers which young children are not aware of, but which adults have learned to avoid. Parents have a duty to teach their children to avoid such dangers as traffic, electricity, poisons, dangerous animals, and other things. A parent has the obligation to say "no" or "don't" if a child approaches any of these hazards. Parents can reduce the need for these negative words, however, by taking reasonable care to minimize the child's exposure to such hazards. Blind plugs can be put into unused electrical outlets. Sharp objects can be kept out of reach. Poisonous detergents and chemicals, as well as all drugs and medicines, can be stored on an inaccessible shelf, and so on.

When you do have to explain to a child why he should not do something that might be dangerous for him, do your best to make sure that he really understands you. Most children do not like to acknowledge that they do not understand words which adults have spoken to them Therefore, if you have any reason to suspect that your child may not understand what you have told him, question him to find out if he knows the meaning of the words you have used. Faced with a direct question, "Do you understand what I mean by base plug?" most children will answer frankly if they do not understand. However, they usually will not volunteer this fact unless you ask them.

To keep children from harming other people or valuable things. The child who hits a playmate with a hard and durable toy should be made to understand clearly that he should not do this again. The child who points a garden hose at his father when father is dressed in a business suit should be made to understand that what may be appropriate for a playmate in a bathing suit does not necessarily apply to father when he is dressed up. The child who picks up and examines a valuable figurine in someone else's home should be made to understand that he should not touch things outside his own home without permission.

Within reasonable limits, children should have the freedom to examine whatever they want in their own homes. This means that parents have the responsibility to keep all dangerous or valuable objects out of reach. However, you should also make it clear to the child that whenever he is out of his own environment, there may be many things he should not touch unless he first gets your permission.

To help the child learn to live in a particular kind of society. Parents have an acculturating duty to perform. They must teach their children to get along in the particular society to which the parents belong or aspire. If you believe it is necessary or desirable for people to say, "How do you do?" "Please," and "Thank you" and for men to rise when ladies enter a room, then it is perfectly reasonable for you to expect this behavior of your child once you have explained to him what you want. But an even more important condition is that you practice this kind of behavior yourself.

A mother and her nine-year-old child got on a city bus. The rule was (and the mother knew it) that children above the age of six must pay a fare. When the mother and her daughter started to get off the bus, the bus driver reminded the mother that she had not paid for the child, whereupon the mother began to berate the driver in a loud and screeching voice that could be heard at the back of the bus, while her child stood by in embarrassment. The mother's actions probably had more effect upon the child's later behavior than any lecture she might have given her daughter about proper public behavior.

For the parents' benefit. Parents are people, and therefore have rights just as children do. A mother who is worn out and suffering from a cold is perfectly justified in asking the children to do some quiet activity, like coloring in a book, while she takes a nap. There is nothing wrong with father shooing some noisy eight-year-olds outside on a sunny afternoon so he can watch a football game on television.

Justified commands need not be peremptory, however. Mother can explain that she badly needs a nap, and must have quiet for an hour or so. Father can explain that he has been looking forward to this football game for a long time, and that he would like to enjoy it. The children may watch it, too, if they promise to be quiet. Parents should not be too demanding, however, in obedience requests that are for their own benefit, unless they wish to teach their children to be demanding, too.

Setting an Example

As with so many other aspects of a child's life, the habits of obedience and discipline begin to be formed in babyhood, and continue through childhood. Parents are the children's main models. Fathers should bear this in mind when mothers ask them to mow the lawn. Quick and cheerful compliance—not growling and complaining—will be noticed by the child, and will be a model for his own behavior in responding to requests. When fathers ask mothers to hurry and get ready for a dinner engagement, mothers should comply without dawdling if they do not wish to rear dawdling children who are never on time.

78

Habits of truthfulness, honesty, and respect for law are also taught by parents more by example than by lecture or admonition. The father who returns from a trip and brags about bribing a policeman into not giving him a ticket for going through a traffic light will undo much that teachers (and possibly even he himself) have tried to do to instill respect for law in his child. If the father then pulls hotel towels from his suitcase, he will give his child an example that taking what does not belong to you is perfectly all right so long as you do not get caught.

The plea above is for some consistency between what parents *say* and what they *do*. Parents should also demonstrate some consistency in what they demand of their children. The child who is permitted to play baseball in his school clothes before dinner on Monday should not be punished for doing the same thing on Tuesday. The child who is cheered and applauded for showing off before relatives should not be smacked for doing the same thing the next day in a restaurant. Such inconsistency on the part of parents will leave the child hopelessly confused and uncertain of how to behave. Therefore, if you make a rule for your child, make sure that it is always obeyed. If you allow the rule to be broken occasionally, like staying up late on a special night, make sure that the child knows this is an exception and that he understands why you are temporarily setting the rule aside.

Wrong Ways of Discipline

Do not use bribes and threats as means of discipline. There is a great temptation for parents to bribe or threaten their offspring, but both of these tactics can lead to very bad consequences. One big trouble with bribes is that they tend to escalate, with the child demanding more and more as he grows older. This can make him avaricious and spoiled. Furthermore, bribing establishes precisely the wrong basis for proper behavior. It makes his proper behavior conditional upon a reward, rather than freely given because his parents ask it of him. Empty threats turn out to be useless as soon as a child comes to realize they will not be carried out. Threats that are carried out serve the child as a model for learning how to get his own way when dealing with someone smaller. This can lead him to become a bully.

One mother who consistently bribed her children was required to institute a rigorous program of physical exercises with one of her girls for medical reasons. The girl refused to do the exercises. Bribes had no effect on her, because she disliked the exercises more than she liked any of the rewards that were offered to her. Yet the doctor insisted that the exercises be done each day. The distraught mother was driven to vigorous spanking, and screams and violent crying were the result. Everyone in the household was upset for more than a month until the girl realized that she *had* to do the exercises; there was no way out of it.

The Question of Spanking

In any discussion of discipline, the subject of spanking must necessarily arise. Karl S. Bernhardt, Director of the

Institute of Child Study, University of Toronto, states: "To inflict pain deliberately on a young child cannot be justified on any grounds." Dr. Spock is not so sure, and feels that spanking might even be helpful at times.

Probably a few judiciously placed whacks can sometimes have a beneficial effect on both the spanker and the spankee. The spanker knows that he has made his point abundantly clear, and in most cases the spanking closes the matter as far as he is concerned. The spankee, though he may be crying, grudgingly respects the parent's firmness, and knows that his punishment is now over and that he will not have to face being deprived of a toy, a dessert, or possibly a Saturday afternoon movie.

But to be effective, spanking should be immediate, in the opinion of many child guidance counselors. A child who runs into the street in defiance of orders should be spanked as soon as he sets foot off the curb, not half an hour later when he and the parent get back home. This is the principle of "reinforcement," which psychologists say should take place within three seconds to be fully effective. Therefore, if you do spank, do it the instant the child commits the transgression. Do not postpone it until father gets home in the evening.

Another good rule to follow is not to spank your child when you are enraged. This commandment may seem to

be in conflict with the rule stated in the paragraph above, but if you do feel enraged with your child, it might be better not to spank but to choose some other form of punishment. If you consistently spank your child when you are in fury, you may be demonstrating to him that the use of physical violence in time of stress or anger is justified and permissible. Such a belief could lead the child to incredible troubles later in life.

So, when you spank a child, if you do, try to be calm and composed. If great fear or anger make composure impossible, hold back your hand and rely on words.

The first duty of a parent is to make himself unnecessary. Parents begin their role as parents with a tiny bawling infant who can do nothing for himself and who is totally dependent on them. When they turn this child out into the world some 18 or 21 years later, if they have fulfilled their role, they have helped transform this helpless infant into a self-sufficient, self-reliant adult who, though he may continue to love them, will have no further need or dependence on them. One of the tools in accomplishing this job is discipline, but an even more important tool is love. Discipline untempered by love is harsh and tyrannical, and, in the long run, ineffective. Discipline that is tempered by love is firm, just, and understanding.

TEACHING PROPER MANNERS

THE MOTHER WENT TO THE DOOR to greet a friend whom she had not seen for a number of years. After effusive doorway greetings, the mother and her guest came into the living room. Seated on a chair, dressed in a crisp, clean dress, was six-year-old Linda.

"Linda," said her mother, "this is Mrs. Walton. Say hello to Mrs. Walton, Linda."

Linda swung her legs over the edge of the chair and stared at the floor.

"Linda," said her mother again. "I asked you to say hello to Mrs. Walton."

Linda continued to stare at the floor.

The mother's tone took on an edge of anger. "Linda, say hello to Mrs. Walton."

"Hi!" said Linda. She got down from the chair and walked out of the room. Before the little girl was out of earshot, her mother said in an exasperated tone, "I don't know how you teach manners to children these days. They just have no respect for older people at all." Mrs. Walton, who was embarrassed by the episode, had the good grace to keep silent.

Parents want their children to learn and use proper manners for a number of reasons. They know that children who practice good manners generally tend to be liked, and those who have bad manners generally are not liked. They recognize that manners are a kind of social lubricant that help to make human affairs run more smoothly. They feel, too, that the manners which their children exhibit reflect directly on them. They also want their children to learn proper manners so that the children will fit into the level of society to which the parents belong or aspire.

Karl S. Bernhardt, Director of the Institute of Child Study, University of Toronto, wrote that, "Manners, like many other features of human activity, are caught more than taught." This has been rather common advice for parents in teaching their children manners. The theory is that if the parents consistently exhibit good manners, it will naturally follow that their children will, too.

This hoped-for result does not always occur. Manners are basically an artificial form of behavior, and therefore must be taught. After all, what is considered good manners in one society may be considered very improper in another. Belching after a meal, for example, is considered very bad manners in the U.S., but is looked upon as a compliment to the host in certain Arabic countries. Demonstrating good manners unquestionably is helpful in teaching children manners, but in itself it will not necessarily guarantee that the children will imitate them. On the other hand, giving children an example of consistently *bad* manners is almost guaranteed to produce a reasonably exact copy of such undesirable behavior!

The basis for most of the behavior that is considered good manners in Western society is consideration for others. "Please," "Thank you," helping ladies put on their coats, or holding doors open for them are primarily based on consideration for the comfort or feelings of others. There-

84

fore, if parents practice these considerations—not just in public or when guests are in the home, but also in private when only the family is present—it will do much to influence their children to have consideration for others, too.

Consideration for others is something that must be taught. It is natural for children to be self-centered and to be concerned primarily with their own wants and desires. Indeed it is considered a mark of maturity when an individual begins to be less self-centered, to think less about himself, and to think more about others. Therefore, the examples of good manners that parents can show toward each other and toward other adults can be of great help to the child in learning manners.

Perhaps even more important are the good manners that parents use toward the child. The mother who shouts to a child at the table, "Eat your meal this instant or leave the table!" probably would never dream of issuing the same command to an adult visitor. Children are acutely aware of these differences, and frequently notice that their parents exhibit a double standard of behavior. To children, it must often appear that one set of manners is being used with outsiders, and a quite different set with them. (If you have any doubts about this, listen to your little girl scolding her doll or to your little boy giving orders to his dog.) Parents should try to remember to be as courteous to their children as they are to each other, and as courteous to their children

as they would like their children to be with them. This means, of course, toning down peremptory commands and being respectful of your children just as you would wish them to be of you. There will be times when the desire to be respectful toward your children will come into conflict with your need to discipline them. These circumstances will not be too difficult to explain to your children provided you have been reasonably consistent and genuine in your display of proper manners toward them.

Most parents would not dream of rebuking a spouse in public or in the presence of guests. The same good sense should govern your encounters with your children. Do not comment on your child's bad manners or embarrass him by calling attention to his social indiscretions in public or in the presence of visitors. If possible, try not even to look strained when your child innocently tells a visitor that her hair looks funny. Save these moments of correction for a private session between you and the child. Then you can explain to him why his comment was inconsiderate and how he might have hurt another person's feelings. If you take care of these indiscretions in private, you will not embarrass your child nearly so much as if you do it in public. You will also be demonstrating to him the same sort of consideration that you want him to exercise toward others.

TEACHING MONEY MANAGEMENT

CHILDREN DEVELOP different attitudes toward money. These attitudes are probably largely determined by the environment in which the children are brought up, and by parents, relatives, friends, and neighbors.

In some homes, money is the scale by which the value of every person or thing is measured. There is constant talk about money. Parents discuss how much a neighbor probably earns or what his property may be worth. Father boasts about how much money he expects to get from the job or sale he just completed. Mother talks about how much a new kitchen appliance will cost or how much she can save if she buys a dress on sale. A child brought up in such a home may feel that acquiring money is the major goal in life and that the amount of money he gets determines his ·success or failure. If he does not feel that piling up money is a goal in itself, the child may regard it as a prize awarded for playing a game well. To such a child, money may come to be viewed as a by-product of his behavior and a proof of his cleverness.

In other homes, there is little talk about money. The parents seldom discuss finances in the presence of their children. Money is considered necessary and desirable, but other interests come first. These may include education, art, music, science, politics, and community service. Leading a relaxed, comfortable, and interesting life is considered more worthwhile than acquiring money. A child brought up in such a home may never have a strong interest in money, since he tends to reflect his parents' attitude toward it.

Besides the attitudes toward money shown by parents and others, the availability of money is another important factor that affects children's attitudes toward money. In some homes, money is never a problem. There always seems to be enough to take care of the essentials and whatever else is wanted—a new car, a pleasant vacation, or a color television set. The father has a good salary and perhaps other income from investments. A child brought up in such a home may feel that money just naturally exists. Certainly, it is nothing that he need worry about. In more homes, however, money is usually a problem and often a very serious one. There is not enough to go around, and it is hard to pay the family's bills. Sometimes, to make ends meet, both parents must work or one parent has two jobs. A child brought up in such a home may feel that security and happiness are impossible without money. He may worry about money much of the time.

New Attitudes Toward Money

The parents' past experiences with money problems can be still another factor affecting children's attitudes toward money. However, this factor tends to lose its force as the experience is forgotten. During the great depression of the 1930's, millions of people were out of work and could obtain little money except from charity or the government. Many of those who had money lost it when banks failed and investments became worthless. For years afterwards, people were concerned with saving, on getting along with as little as possible, and on not spending money unless absolutely necessary. But by the 1960's, a new generation of young adults had grown up, and only their parents or grandparents remembered the great depression.

Today, buying on credit has become a way of life for many people. They rely on borrowing money and paying it back over a period of months or years. Credit cards and quick loans are easily obtained from stores, banks, and other business firms. Installment buying, once considered dangerous, has become an accepted practice. Newspaper advertisements and radio and television commercials constantly urge people to buy now and pay later. Children are urged to persuade their parents to buy this or that toy, candy, toothpaste, or breakfast food. It is no wonder that today's parents have a hard time deciding what to teach their children about money management.

Your Child's Allowance

Among child psychologists, family counselors, home economists, and others who have thought and written about money management, there seems to be general agreement that parents should train their children to cope with the conditions that exist today. Practically all of these experts advise parents to give their children opportunities to learn how to handle money by giving each child a regular allowance when he is five, six, or seven years old. The exact starting age will vary with the child and will depend, for one thing, on how well he understands the value of the various coins. It will also depend on the kind of place in which he lives. A child who lives in a house in a small community and who can trot around the corner to the store by himself may begin spending his own money sooner than a child who lives in a big apartment building in a large city and is seldom allowed outdoors alone.

To start with, the child's allowance should be small, probably no more than 25 to 50 cents a week. The younger the child, the smaller the amount should be. As the child gets older and his real needs for money increase, his allowance should be increased accordingly.

Parents should be prepared for some early disappointments. A young child has great difficulty in deferring pleasures. Quite often, he will be tempted to spend an entire week's allowance the first time he has a chance. If he is to learn from this experience, the best thing that his parents can do is to let him have his way. Then they should point out that he will not be able to buy anything else for the rest of the week. They must stick to this position, no matter how much the child pleads for more money a few days later. Otherwise he will never learn to pace his demands and to plan for future expenditures.

Once the parents have agreed to give a child a regular allowance, it should always be paid on time. The child's behavior should not be made a condition of payment. To make the giving or withholding of an allowance conditional on the child's behavior is in effect using the money as a bribe. In the long run, this practice is self-defeating, because a child soon learns to demand more and more money for his continuing good behavior. Parents should also not use money to bribe a child into earning better grades in school. A child who becomes accustomed to such bribes is likely to become too money-minded. He may even turn into a bargainer who is never willing to do anything unless he is paid for it. He may thus be robbed of self-reliance and other important values that his parents want to teach him.

90

Moreover, children should not be paid for every job they do around the home. Even in this day of labor-saving devices, there are still many duties to be performed. Parents have every right to insist that their children assume a fair share of the work. Routine chores such as setting or clearing the table, making the beds, disposing of garbage, and caring for family pets can be assigned to children, depending on their age and ability. Children should be expected to perform these daily jobs without pay. However, parents may quite properly pay children for doing special jobs such as washing the windows, mopping the floors, or polishing the furniture. If a child wants to buy something (a bicycle or a pair of skates, for example) that is well beyond his allowance, his parents may arrange for him to earn the extra money by doing special jobs. He will probably value his purchase even more because he worked to earn it himself.

One more aspect of teaching money management deserves mention. Parents should help their children learn to weigh and test advertising claims. There is perhaps no sadder sight than a child who has worked and saved to buy something that appears glamorous but turns out to be worthless junk. All of us—children and adults alike—are continually bombarded with appeals to buy all sorts of things, some necessary, some desirable, still others a waste of money. How to decide? Children, with their limited experience, quite understandably do not always make sound judgments in money matters. And, because of poor training, some adults do little better than children. Therefore, it should be the responsibility of parents to set a good example by evaluating advertising claims and spending their own money as wisely as possible.

HOW TO HELP YOUR

CHILD USE THIS SET

THE HOME ADVENTURE LIBRARY has been carefully planned for children aged four to ten. Actually this is a fairly broad age range, because it includes at one end of the scale preschool children who cannot yet read but are being read to by their parents, and at the other end of the scale, children who are independent readers and have in many cases developed strong interests in one subject or another.

The needs of both groups are very much alike in some ways, however. For one thing, both four-year-olds and ten-year-olds seem to prefer stories or chapters that are fairly short rather than long expository books. For this reason each of the volumes in this set is made up of a number of fairly brief but complete and self-contained chapters. The set is also liberally illustrated with color pictures that add excitement and visual appeal.

Parents of non-readers can read a chapter or two from one of the books to a child at bedtime or whenever the child wishes to be read to. Each chapter in every book is self-contained and does not require knowledge of preceding chapters. Therefore, you can skip around among the volumes, and select chapters which will appeal to your child.

The books can also be read in a similar way by children in the primary grades who are independent readers. Since these books are meant primarily for leisure time reading, the child can dip into any book that interests him at any point that he wishes. He can also begin at the beginning and read a book all the way through.

It is not likely that every chapter in all of the books will be of equal interest to your child. However, the range of subject matter in these volumes is so great that certainly a great many of the chapters will be of immediate interest to him. Others will intrigue him as he gets a little older.

Book 1. The Earth and the Stars
Most of the chapters in this book will be of great interest to preschoolers and to primary grade children. The chapter titled "When the Earth was Young" will fascinate any child at bedtime, as will the chapters "What Ancient People Thought About Space," "Our Sun," "Our Moon," "Neighbors in Space," and "Will You Travel in Space?" Many of the other chapters in this book will reinforce and supplement what an older child is learning in school courses in earth-space science.

Book 2. Numbers and Discoveries
This book contains stories about famous men of science, and articles about various branches of science. The stories about Archimedes, Leeuwenhoek, and Newton are fascinating reading for a preschooler or a ten-year-old. The articles on "Alchemists Search for Gold," "Ancient Medicine," and "New Sciences" will also interest young children as well as older ones. The articles on "Heat," "Light," "Sound," and "The World of Chemistry" contain intriguing information about everyday phenomena that children and adults take for granted as they encounter daily scientific "miracles."

Book 3. Plants and Animals

All children are interested in plants and animals, and the attractive illustrations in this book help to make it particularly informative. Young children have shown particular interest in the chapters on "Smallest Plants," "Biggest Plants," "Smallest Animals," and "Biggest Animals." They are also very much interested in the article on "Ancient Animals," because this chapter includes information about dinosaurs which seem to have universal appeal for children. Children in the third and fourth grades will find the articles on "Plant Families," "Animal Families," and the section on "Natural Communities" to be of particular help to them in their school work.

Book 4. People and Places

This is primarily a book of world history told in a number of stories about famous people and famous places, from early primitive man down to the twentieth century. The stories are entertainingly but also accurately recounted, and nearly all of them will appeal to preschool as well as to ten-year-old children. If a child shows special interest in one or more of these stories, you can find additional books in the library dealing with this period of history which will carry his interest farther.

Book 5. America's Story

This book presents the saga of America as told in a series of stories about famous people and events that shaped our history. The story of the Jamestown colony is here, and the story of the landing of the Pilgrims at Plymouth Rock. There is a detailed description of colonial life, stories about the American Revolution, and about fascinating American characters like Johnny Appleseed, the Wright Brothers, and Mathew Brady. Children will learn what frontier life was like, about steamboat days on the Mississippi, about the Civil War, life in the Old West and even about such modern events as the Korean War and the story of the Green Berets in Vietnam. Like the other books, this book need not be read from start to finish. Each chapter is self-contained, and you can pick and choose among them to find the ones that your child will like best.

Book 6. All About You

This book is a fascinating introduction to a child of the wonders of his own body. Try reading the first chapter, "The Miracle of You," to a preschooler, and if he shows interest, read him all of the rest of the book one chapter at a time. This book also contains very informative and helpful sections on "Keeping Fit," "Health Rules," and "Good Grooming." These chapters will be of particular help to older children.

Book 7. Great Stories from World Literature

This book contains many old favorites that have been loved by children for generations, but which are not often seen today. Fairy tales like "The Frog Prince" and "The Nightingale," and adventure stories like *The Merry Adventures of Robin Hood* and *Treasure Island* are appealing to children of all ages. Younger children will also enjoy hearing over and over again the fables and Mother Goose rhymes. And older children will laugh with Tom Sawyer as he feeds painkiller to his Aunt Polly's cat.

Book 8. Holidays and Entertaining

This book is divided into three sections: "American Holidays," "Holidays Throughout the World," and "Parties and Entertaining." Young children who are being read to will enjoy hearing about American holidays, how they came to be, and why they are observed as they are. They will also be fascinated hearing about customs in other lands that have grown up around Easter, Christmas, and other religious holidays. All children will enjoy reading about the unusual holidays that are observed in many different parts of the world. When it comes time to plan your child's birthday party, you and he can go through the "Parties" section and together plan the invitations, games, and refreshments. Party behavior and manners are also described.

Book 9. Fact Book and Index

This is a diamond mine of interesting information, attractively arranged and organized so that children can understand it. Children will have great fun browsing through this unusual book, absorbing the fascinating information it contains. This book also contains a sports section with rules for baseball, football, and basketball. These rules have been especially adapted for children.

This book also contains a combined index to all of the volumes in this set. For each entry two numbers are given (for example, **Skin, 6:53**). The first numeral indicates the volume number of the book, and the second, the page number in that book where the information will be found. Teach your child how to use this index and remind him to use it whenever he wants to find specific information. Learning to use reference materials is an important study skill which your child will need to use throughout his career in school.